THE AMERICAN HIGH SCHOOL BAND

THE AMERICAN HIGH SCHOOL BAND

By

George Taylor

RICHARDS ROSEN PRESS, INC.
New York, N.Y. 10010

Published in 1977 by Richards Rosen Press, Inc.
29 East 21st Street, New York, N.Y. 10010

First edition

Library of Congress Cataloging in Publication Data

Taylor, George H
  The American high school band.

1. Bands (Music)—Instruction and study.
I. Title.
MT733.T35   785′.06′707   76–58476
ISBN 0–8239–0387–7

Manufactured in the United States of America

ABOUT THE AUTHOR

GEORGE TAYLOR has had broad experience in The Band—as player, director,
and adjudicator. A graduate of Sher-
wood School of Music and Virginia
State College, he attended DePaul,
Marshall, Eastern Kentucky, and
Morehead universities, the University
of Wisconsin, and the College of William and Mary. He holds the degrees
of Bachelor of Music and Master of
Music Education.

Currently directing band in Michigan, he has headed bands
that have won superior festival ratings in West Virginia and
Ohio. He was formerly Coordinator of Instrumental Music for
the Hopewell (Virginia) City Schools. Under his twelve-year
directorship the Hopewell High School Band grew into a 135-
piece symphonic/marching powerhouse. The famous Blue Devil
Band received many festival awards and trophies for its music
and its parade precision and was noted for thrilling half-time
drills and colorful extravaganza shows.

Mr. Taylor played trombone in high school, in the Hunting-
ton Symphony, and in USAAF marching and dance bands, and
he led his own jazz bands in Ohio and West Virginia. He served
on the three-man committee that established the Virginia Stage
Band Festival. He was first among music educators to offer stage
band and guitar as credit classes in the school curriculum.

Mr. Taylor has published articles in magazines in the United
States and seven foreign countries. For years his column on

v

music and the arts, "The Human Tide," appeared weekly in the Hopewell *News* and was syndicated in other Southern newspapers. His professional affiliations include membership in the National Association of Jazz Educators, the Michigan Band and Orchestra Directors' Association, the WEA, the MEA, and the NEA. He is an experienced adjudicator of stage bands, concert bands, and parade band festivals.

PREFACE

This book is for students in American high school bands. It explores the band world for those ready to join, and it may expand the scene for those who are already bandsmen. It shows all the exciting rewards awaiting student bandsmen. *The Band* is an endless, revolving three-ring circus.

The band offers something for everyone. Some students join for fun and enjoyment; for them, the yearly activity calendar of band offers variety and excitement. Other students may look for thrills and spectacle, or glitter and glamour set to music. Bandsmen with real musical talent find achievement, recognition, and often lasting rewards in musical careers.

The ideas and suggestions in this book apply equally wherever one joins the band. Both rural scene and city hustle unite as one. The band experience is universal. *The Band* is a world all its own.

It is a life of thrill and music; the variety of sports spectaculars and parades, of trips and concerts. It is an opportunity for musical exploration and for the creation of lifelong friendships in an unbroken circle of things to do and places to go.

There is an old saying about music and *The Band:* "One does not choose music or *The Band. The Band* claims its own."

AUTHOR'S NOTE

As a high school band director I have spent twenty years waving a conductor's baton over the musical lives of thousands of fine bandsmen whom I shall never forget, and who, in turn, will never forget those memorable "good old days" in their high school band.

The concepts and suggestions stated herein are not the dry theories commonly found in books by stodgy educators. Rather, they are valid observations and ideas drawn from life and my own firsthand experience in bands and instrumental music.

After all these years I still think it's the most rewarding "racket" in the world.

As a school bandsman I made lifelong friends in the band, fell in love in the band, and finally *with* the band, and the honeymoon with it has never ended.

All I ask for my last ride is: spare me the plaintive hymnal tunes, or the somber, measured tread of funeral drums. Instead, let my high school band swing along behind the hearse with all my old band students or their ghosts blasting away like a powerhouse, reaching the far, green hills with something full of pep and jazz like "High Society," or "Lordy! Didn't He Ramble!"

GEORGE TAYLOR

ACKNOWLEDGMENTS

For many of the photographs in this book I wish to thank the *Creative World* of Stan Kenton; Ray Dickenson of Utica, Michigan; Don Nawrocki, band director of the Utica (Michigan) high school band; Bill Minor, photographer, of Roanoke, Virginia; and the U.S. Navy.

All other photographs are by the author.

CONTENTS

Rewards • Relationships with the Student Body • Faculty
Members • Band Booster Club • Civic Groups

Contents

THE AMERICAN HIGH SCHOOL BAND

I

WHIRLIGIG

The world of the high school band is the most thrilling one a school bandsman may ever have. It is a time of excitement and of things happening. The rewards for playing in the band can be immediate, but they have lasting effects as well. The cultural and critical appreciation for music lasts a lifetime.

The purpose of this book is to crystallize the "school band world." It portrays the scene for those about to enter, and it should broaden the subject for those already in band. It seeks to show the band world in all its glorious sound and fury.

The Special Quality of the Bandsman's World

No one reaches a destination without noticing the surrounding landscape along the way. The same is true for music or band. Each student has goals or aims in band. This book may serve as a digest of what the band student can expect, or it may reveal what he should receive but often does not.

There is no national bureau of standards for the American high school band. The Music Educators National Conference does not seek to do its utmost for the band program in America.

The highest official level of school "banddom" are the various state departments of music. Most states have some type of annual band contest or festival. Their slant and results are more historic than relevant, however. Progressiveness in educational circles has never really extended to "the band."

Those states controlling band have regional screening. These local festivals serve to separate the common from the uncommon. A final, higher judgment called "adjudication" comes at state festivals. This experience can be musically rewarding. For most band students, however, the rewards are questionable. Then, too, band-director politics enters the picture when the adjudicator grades are released.

The state and regional band festivals often stifle the musically advanced bandsman. Such students chafe at the musical bit, and with good reason! Three or four months of intense work lead to the contest itself.

A long- drawn-out analysis of three or four contest selections of dubious musical value turns off many good band students. It may be that the American band has expended all the effort it needs in the present festival program. New times demand new approaches and even new music. New ideas are so rare that they usually are rejected when they appear. This may be one of the reasons they so seldom appear. It certainly is why the band-festival system has lasted so long, and it may indicate that it will remain with us for a long time to come.

Most good music students and enthusiastic bandsmen want to hurry on to new musical explorations. They should be both allowed and encouraged to do so. In fact, it is one of the band director's chief responsibilities to lead them into such exploration.

The Color and the Spectacle

Every American parade is a spangled rainbow of multicolored uniforms glimpsed through furling flags. High-stepping majorettes amid billowing banners add to the thrills of sight and sound. The throb of drums and piercing brassy voice of horns is enough to make the American "man in the street" throw down his crutch or leap from his wheelchair and fly aloft on wings of music when the band goes down the street.

The high, soaring melody of the trumpets alone is enough to arouse a quiver in the most calloused heart. It is all enough to

Parading through Colonial Williamsburg, these majorettes show off the street routines they have practiced all summer.

bring a lump in the throat and misty eyes to all patriots as the band thunders while the flags go by.

Growth and Achievement

All this and musical and cultural growth for the bandsman, too? Yes, it is possible. The pressure of public performance weighs heavy on the band. It is even heavier on the band director. In one sense, this pressure can be disturbing and confining. On the other hand, it is a decisive influence on the musical and technical growth of the bandsman.

A public performance on the musical horizon spurs the student on to greater things. His intensive effort to favorably impress family and friends leads to musical growth and achievement. Public recognition is not a small thing. The performance, the preparation for it, frenzied or otherwise, and the result are all part of musicianship.

Musicianship is an elusive quality, yet all music students strive or should strive for it. It is not a fringe benefit; it is the main attraction. Musicianship is the core and being of band.

For these reasons, a band should be performance-oriented. This has long been a subject for debate among band directors and college-level educators. Actually, some band directors fear public performance, and they take advantage of whatever negative aspects of public performance there may be.

Some of these directors perceive their role and that of their band as that of "seriously studying music," whereas the performance band is a motley crew of noisemakers. These "hothouse flowers" view performance as an evil that takes time from their serious study of music. The argument of such directors is that the study and rehearsal in the band room is the means *and* the end.

Actually, a band trapped in such a musical vacuum is being robbed of its rightful heritage, to say nothing of its fun.

No parent or booster group will support such a shrinking violet for long, and they shouldn't. A public performance is proof of the pudding. Who knows what goes on in a band room if the results are never heard? Band is exciting. It should be. It involves private practice, of course; but that should be pointed toward playing in public.

The Band as a National Phenomenon

Many new students enter band with a foggy picture of what it is all about. They don't know how it fits into the larger American music scene. The place of the band should be of great interest to the above-average bandsmen. Every band director hopes to attract only students who are above average. This is a misguided hope in every respect. What is average?

First-year band members are so involved that they have no time to concern themselves with facts or figures. But statistics reveal a great deal about American high school bands. Instrumental music in the schools of America is extensive.

A band student may be surprised to know that his band is one of thirty thousand or forty thousand in America. It should comfort a band student to know that he is not alone in his love of music. His band is not merely an object of curiosity and noise. The band movement in this country is vital. It runs deep in our economy. It is widely cross-grained. It includes student members of every race, creed, color, and religion on the face of the earth. As such, it is a microcosmic America in uniform dazzling the eyes and warming the hearts of millions. The program loosely known as The American High School Band is like Topsy: it was not planned or structured toward growth. Instead, it "just grew."

The band as we know it is an open-ended institution. And, like all institutions with the passage of time, it has sailed its musical seas only to run aground on the shoals of "relevancy."

Although the band is an institutional organ, and a giant one at that, it is more. It is a turbulent, living organism struggling to pay homage to an illustrious past. But this ancestry may have more historic than musical value. The struggle is in trying at the same time to reflect the flavor and timbre of the times.

A Mirror of the Times

Today's band must accurately reflect the fabric of current American musical life. If it chooses to do otherwise, it may shortly find itself scattered to the four winds.

The idea that a band be a mirror of public times is neither trifling nor obscure. The first bands reflected their times and founders. The question of how relevant a band should be is not new. Bands have always been tied to the times of their existence.

What is new is the tenor of our life and times. Somehow,

bands must survive the solid-state, amplified world of approaching deafness. If they are to continue through this day of thunderous decibels, they must take on some tough new fiber. They need new color and some as yet unidentified dimension.

Economic Impact

Aside from music, the high school band world is vital to the national economy. Millions of high school musicians are super-buyers in their purchases in the music field. Instruments and music as well as repairs and other support machinery are necessary, available, bought, and sold in the marketplace.

The buying and selling by all these millions of high school students has a staggering impact on America's financial structure. Millions of people buying in the marketplace circulate billions of dollars. As any fund-raising bandsman soon learns, a hundred dollars is hard to accumulate in a sales campaign. A billion staggers the imagination. Economically, the American school band must continue to grow and flourish. But that is not the only reason it must.

The great service performed by the high school band is that it links together a solid chain of American musical life and culture. This applies both to performers and to appreciative audience.

Thousands of bands produce millions of performers, advanced students, and other also-rans. But it pours the greatest numbers into a vast body of musical consumers. Bands produce the buyers of records, albums, and record players. Former bandsmen buy the sophisticated sound equipment, tape recorders, and tickets to symphony concerts.

Band, however, is so imbedded in the American mainstream that its power is overlooked. Without the presence of American high school bands, America's musical life would be radically different and greatly weakened. From our school bands come our best future performers. They move on up through the music departments of universities or colleges. Others go into music schools or conservatories for professional training.

Eventually they reappear in our best dance bands, superior rock or recording groups, or symphony orchestras. Some go on to become stars as soloists. Some become leaders of bands and orchestras. Strong talent always finds a way.

Native American musical composers are few. Good ones are rare. Great ones are practically nonexistent. The native genius that will give America its great native classical music has not yet appeared.

II

INTERESTING FACTS ABOUT BAND

It Happens Every August

That is when most good bands begin. The specter of approaching pigskin pageantry rises early to haunt every high school band and director alike. It comes before the tag end of summer fades away.

Some schools open officially in late August, others after Labor Day. In both cases, bands of any stature or prominence in their communities have worked a hard two, three, or even four weeks before the opening of school. Some bands have already played in a Labor Day Parade when school opens.

Getting ready for the football shows must begin as early as possible. Bands whose trademark is precision drill will have practiced for weeks in some weed-choked dusty drill field long before their classmates have even cracked a book.

Audience Support

In most places all eyes are on the football team, but all ears are tuned in to hear what the band has to say musically that season. Not that quality is demanded; it is usually not expected on the gridiron.

But this indifference on the part of stadium audiences should not affect the good director. It should not keep the better band from striving for good tonal quality. It should have little to do with the effort toward musical section balance. Yet such a band could well be preparing a show fit for national televised football games.

This drum major leads a spirited band that has worked hard for two months
to make a good showing in an early autumn parade.

In fact, a smart director and a good, responsive band can
kill two musical birds with one stone. It is not easy, and it demands the utmost from all concerned. But the pride and esteem
of a major audience is not to be ignored. The crowd in the football stadium is a major captive audience for a high school band.
Its attention and support should be sought with cold calcula-
tion. A band may put on a show that pleases even the crudest
stadium audience, yet at the same time it is possible to upgrade
the quality of musical fare offered to that same group. All that
is required is careful, methodical, long-range planning. The
director does the planning. The band carries out its part faith-
fully.

The August musical merry-go-round does not run down for
the high school band when the football season ends. The tune

changes, and so does the scene. Football fades as basketball begins. Christmas comes and cold parades on snow-packed avenues call the band. In fact, it is on call until the last book of the school year has been closed. And even after the last student has faded away into the welcome oblivion of June, the band may still have obligations. A regatta parade? Fourth of July celebration? There is no end.

Nobody in school puts in a longer year than the band; therefore, dividends from each activity are desirable. They should be sought actively by all band students and directors.

Most bands christen the school year with a Labor Day parade or a football half-time show. This first show is often an act of sheer desperation by nervous bandsmen.

At first glance, a Labor Day parade seems a good idea. It opens the fall season. It begins things. But although such a parade is colorful to the sideline audience, it can often be a disaster. Many bands do not have time to prepare adequately for such an event. But the demands of communities on their bands call for the utmost. Everyone concerned must practice and cooperate to the fullest before a decent showing is possible.

Every experienced bandsman wants to be a member of a large, well-regarded band, an accomplished combination marching-concert unit. But such an accomplished band calls for student talent. It demands blood, sweat, and tears. The students and director often must work themselves to exhaustion to produce a desired result. It also requires brains and talent, and some directors and bands suffer in this area.

Administrative Problems

To build a good band today requires all the brains a director can muster. He often finds an insurmountable object in his administrator.

A surprising number of administrators and guidance departments take a dim view of band, seeing little value in the band experience. To them, anyone can "make noise" in the band. In schools where this philosophy is strong, the bands are less than they could or should be. In some such bands perhaps 40 percent of the membership is there because there was simply "nowhere else to schedule them."

This is an all too common struggle for band directors today. It is ridiculous. The long, colorful, and inspiring heritage of today's high school band did not develop toward such a demeaning end. But many guidance counselors and principals see band as an academic stepchild, the first and perhaps sole depository for disciplinary problem students. There, at least, "they can make noise and cause no trouble."

The trouble the band director faces in such a situation is immediate and insoluble.

Gaining a Good Image

Public esteem is the prime goal of a fine director. It is the foundation of top bands. Without it the band will perish. Without great community appreciation and pride the school band cannot exist. Without esteem and recognition, it cannot function as a satisfying musical unit.

Public pride has a chain reaction. If the football-show band gets a weak reaction from the stadium audience, the band members have no esprit de corps. Without self-pride, they will not try to achieve a more desirable image. Negative audience reaction drags down bandsman concern. It causes the most talented students to avoid band like the plague. They run, not walk, as they hurry off to join the dramatics club, debating team, or table tennis tournament. In no time the band crumbles away. The bewildered director beats a hasty retreat while he wonders what on earth happened?

New band directors may well ask, "And what, pray tell, creates the desired image? Or, how do I reach nirvana with an audience?"

This majorette corps builds goodwill by working with the cheerleaders in a combined stadium routine.

The answer should be self-evident. It is simple but difficult. A band gains the desired image by earning it. There is no other way.

It is true that many bands rank high with their own supportive audience because of ballyhoo. Some directors have a talent for publicity. They lean on it. They train corps of student publicists who turn out reams of publicity. Very infrequently some of it may even be true. But bands with such a philosophy usually are full of sound and fury, signifying nothing musical that one would care to hear in concert.

The Band Director's Problems

Top bands with the image desired by fine directors nearly always have great and loyal support and followings. Such a case is all built on one thing: the longevity of the director. Directors cannot build top bands overnight. Yet this truth is often impossible to be grasped by pushy, impatient parents and musically ignorant citizens. Such incurable optimists usually do not have the foggiest notion of the building problems concerned. A five-year building program is the average required to produce a good band. After such time, it can then level off and concentrate on tonal quality, technical skill, and musical nuance. Until then, the emphasis must be on recruitment.

Top bands with fine reputations result from long construction with one director wielding his musical baton. The most unnoticeable yet most important aspect of top bands is their stability within sections. They have soloists of high ability. They maintain a good overall musical balance. They do not go up and down in size, section, and ability like a musical yoyo. Some bands suffering from a lack of planning by their directors are like reeds in a wind.

Top bands with top reputations receiving high community esteem owe it all to their directors. The director has built the structure toward that end. A fine band merits high pride and esteem when it has a long history of fine public performances. This is impossible without a stable and unfluctuating membership. The sections must maintain a regular balance. There must be a singular focus and effort from one director at the helm.

Therefore, it is important that both director and bandsmen unify their efforts. They must stabilize band membership. This is a serious field of study and effort in itself.

Stable sectional membership and ability are the timbers of organization. They can be supported only by an effective feeder program in which the director keeps his fingers on the pulse. He must be aware of his prospects from the beginner to the pyramid top, the performing band itself.

Administrative leaders are not all alike. Some are loath to acknowledge that a fine band requires a great deal of money. Others are generous with funds, pouring money into new instruments, uniforms, and music. They may be the type, too, who fail to understand why their band numbers a mere twenty-five in a school with two thousand students. The school is only four years old, and they have given the band a new director every year. What is wrong?

Plenty! Money does not build a band, although it is certainly a necessity. Leaving things up to the director of the year does not build a band either. What, then, is the open sesame?

Feeder Program

A solid feeder program in the elementaries is the first answer. This foundation must route section players up the right road, leading into higher levels year by year. There must be a careful screening of talent and ability. The director must restrict the number of personnel in each section. A stable balance must exist within the whole band.

The director must make full plans and be ever watchful. He must nurse his young players along. He must see that they come up through the ranks and reach the last, higher levels in high school years.

The director is the key. He must see to it that his feeder students never stray from the course he has charted. He must outline it, support it, and keep it firm.

Many promising bandsmen are enticed off into fleeting interests. These good folk must be kept on the band track. A top band with a prime image enjoys its reputation because a knowledgeable, hard-working director shaped it toward that goal.

Graduation Losses

Every good school band has a varied and exciting year. Yet, if anything, the director's year is twofold that of his students. It was his to plan, and it was his alone, it often seems, to execute.

A director's work behind the scenes is starkly revealed by his

performing band, however. The community and band supporters hear the band in concert. But what they see and hear is
only the tip of the iceberg. Under the surface there must be a
deep and abiding foundation.

Feeders are busy training replacements. Sections often lose
their best players on graduation day. Graduation losses haunt
every good director beginning the first day of August. To replace
these losses, the director must know who is coming up the
feeder line. Who will be available to replace his graduating
senior trumpet or first trombonist?

Multiply this problem by six or seven band sections. Put a
heavy black question mark above the heads of hundreds of
students in the lower grades. Who is down there with talent?
Who is dependable? Who is serious about his band work? Who
can already play?

These questions give a dim but adequate picture of the director's first and foremost problem. It is a chronic one. The wise
director looks for his chickens long before he needs them. And
he helps them hatch somewhere along the way. They must be
kept in the program if at all possible.

III

THE BAND DIRECTOR

There are two types of football half-time shows. The pageant show is the easier to work up, practice, and perform. Thus it is the most common, and many directors do these only. The result is a common band, duplicated ten thousand times across the land.

Then there is another kind of director, the man who knows precision drill. He teaches it to his band, which becomes a top marching unit, noted for its precision drill figures at half-time.

In fact, the well-drilled precision marching band quickly be-

Even cartwheels and double wheel routines are built on strict eight-count sets.

comes an institution, but an uncommon one. Such a band usually has little competition in its own area. It immediately climbs into prominence and reaps a harvest of pride, esteem, respect, and honors. But behind the great band is the shadow of its director. He must have been a great drill director.

It is obvious that the inexperienced director will avoid the precision drill show. It is difficult to teach and takes many hours of practice to perfect.

In any case, advanced bands of any stature establish an identity with one type of show or the other. Top bands should be praiseworthy in both areas. But in no case will a band and its show be any better than its director.

To handle both types of show capably is an ideal goal, but it requires a broadminded and extremely capable director. It is both fortunate and unfortunate that school bands reflect the director's personal and musical tastes. They also reflect his ability in all areas.

The Director's Dilemma

Often a director builds a top show band that turns out to be weak in concert. The entire community throws bouquets to a band of musicians that falls flat on its musical face at festivals and contests. That is not ideal.

The dilemma for all concerned is clear. It is most evident to the director: he who develops a fine show band may be lambasted. Critical brickbats will be thrown at his contest results or grade. Conversely, he who works to build a top contest and musical-performance band is likely to be run out of town before his second season. Well-meaning, highly indignant football-show fans all demand bigger and better stadium shows. They must be filled with noise, color, spectacle, and more noise.

Little wonder that some band directors remain as such only long enough to earn a degree in administration. Some resort to advanced certificates in stamp collecting. Others quickly desert the noisy field of musical battle. And it is a long one, at that. It begins with the early, rolling thunder of the drums of August. It does not cease until the flood of students and public appearances ebb in June.

Make no mistake, if the bandsman's life is full, complex, and full of problems, the director's is even more so. A fine director's performance calendar begins with a Labor Day parade. Before that has disbanded, the first football show opens what may be a season of ten or twelve half-time shows.

In the midst of football somebody wants to unveil a plaque to some long-forgotten patriot in a distant cow pasture. The band must go. A Halloween carnival, an autumn concert, an Armistice Day parade, a Christmas parade, or a program to greet the new arrivals from Lower Slobovia seems in order.

A winter concert must be prepared. Pop concerts scattered throughout the school year help with the student body. Music must be worked up for these.

Basketball pep band music is in the air. Requests come from the gym direction. Regional and state festival music must be selected. After purchase, it must be assigned and worked on without letup until the contest date rolls around. School dramatics may call for a pit band; can the school band handle this assignment?

The band's own spring concert is there all the time, lurking around the corner. Will the band be prepared? Will the audience like the music? Following the concert, graduation calls for pomp and circumstance. It always helps to have final exams at the same time. Variety is the spice of a bandsman's life.

Thirty-six Public Performances a Year

Some top bands perform as many as thirty-six public performances in a single school year. Those who do are apt to receive requests for thirty-seven the year following and forty-five the next. But an even thirty-six amounts to almost a performance a week.

All this public performance, however, is good. It demands allegiance, attentiveness, good attendance, and plenty of home practice. After a time all this, surprisingly enough, produces the effect desired by many top band directors.

Their band is the top band in the area. It has the finest image and name. It has the highest community support and esteem. But how long can band and director keep up such a schedule?

Such a full calendar is as rigorous as vaudeville. The demands of a present-day television series would be a snap compared to the band director's year.

Community groups and clubs see only their own needs. They politely ignore all other demands prior to or following their own made upon the band. Put them all together, and the director and band all have a killing pace. But it is colorful, it is exciting, it is varied, it keeps them busy, and there is no time to slack off.

The average school year for such a musical organization is an endless string of bright, high-lighted whirl. But it cannot happen successfully unless it is adequately planned.

Preparing for thirty-six public performances a year requires many hours of planning. This background preparation is seldom apparent to the community audience. For this reason, the band director is often greatly misunderstood.

Who Is a Good Director?

Top directors are a combination of many parts. They must be first and foremost musicians of a high order. They must be conductors, ballyhoo artists, con men, fund raisers, recruiters, drill instructors, drum majors, teachers, father-confessors, diplomats, and dictators.

Top bands have fine instrumentalists, students with good attitudes, fine soloists, good music readers, and clowns. Humor is never out of place, unless it be on the concert stage. The students must be publicity-conscious with the sensibilities of concert-masters. It helps if they are inspired musicians as well.

But top bands with top directors are few and far between, and with good reason. How often can a community find or pay a man having all the characteristics of a god and a devil, a slave and a king?

And where, indeed, does a community find students willing to work their coattails off, willing to endure the rigors of the yearly band activity calendar, willing to work year after year with little if any commendation save that from their own director?

Yes, where?

This is why fine bands with fine directors rank with prehistoric monsters. They are in danger of becoming extinct, if they are not already so.

Aside from all these factors, the good director and band today face a common enemy: the shadow of the "uncivil rights" movement launched with such fanfare in the 1960's.

This turmoil and trouble surfaces in many sharply defined organizations. In bands it has become magnified and has even affected the quality of musicianship. The fabric of social relationships existing in band was closely knit. In some bands it has been rent asunder.

Band today is in a state of transition. The same thing could have been said in every era, but today it has a special meaning. Historically the band has no parallel to sustain it in its current hour of need—and the hour is here. In some areas it has already passed. But if the band is in transition, it must lead to something new.

Even the band literature in existence before 1960 is currently held in ill repute or open disdain by many students. At best, better students have visible distaste for its flavor; weak students even more so.

The whole concept of band is changing. Its makeup clearly is in a state of transition. Its unity of attitude is changing. Boundary lines once sharply defined in a fine band have become hazy, stretching off in several directions because of the radical interests of our social fabric today. New horizons are evident among the students themselves.

The whole American high school band picture is more challenging than ever. This presents problems for the director in that it is having a disruptive effect upon the band as an ongoing, organized institution. The band students may be helped by having a clearer picture of the band's inspiring heritage. Band has been a wonderful field peopled with magnificent characters, colorful characters, and great musicians.

Why, then, must such rich background be denigrated in the name of social progress? Social protest is one thing. But it cannot rob the American high school band of its rightful past. What has been accomplished cannot be taken away. Things may change radically, but the rich past of the high school band is there for eternity. Let him judge who will; it will have little effect on what has gone before.

It is callous to throw out the old for the new; to do so serves little purpose and may have much ill effect. To cast off the band's past glory would be catastrophic. Bandsmen would be better off knowing the full meaning of American high school band. If this book helps to fill in the band picture, it will have served a good purpose.

Musical Appreciation

No band worthy of the name can exist solely upon the shaky foundation of today's musical bill of fare. It must necessarily have background and depth. If even the best band students turn up their noses at the musical past, they must be gently led to it at all costs.

Indeed, it will pay and repay a thousand times over to do so. Musical appreciation is a flimsy thread, at best; but the only way to build it in band students is to push forward through the literature. Transient dislike or disdain must be disregarded.

Appreciation builds parallel to confidence in playing skills.

Appreciation for music builds slowly in concert bands, but it is long-lasting for the students.

That which a musician plays well, he loves—in fact, he usually begs to play it again and again. Taste barriers, therefore, must be beaten down. They must be used as structural beams to support and reweave the musical tastes of the present. Out of the old and the new will come a new combination. And who knows what it will be? It may be better than the fare of today and yesterday as well. Is that not worth striving for? Appreciation of beauty in music is a goal worth working for. The road may be new and untried, but has this not always been the case?

IV

MUSICAL APTITUDE AND TALENT

What Is Talent?

Musical talent means special ability in music. But the term is a catchall. The musical world is large and varied. Talent for what? Or in what?

A prospective band student may feel or sense that he has talent. He may have loved music all his life. He may own a room full of popular music albums. He may know every singer and musician alive. He may wish to play an instrument. But what instrument? How does he choose? Is his talent great enough to ensure success on the instrument he finally selects?

There are quick, certain, and more definite ways to sum up his case than to say, "Time will tell" or "Trial and error." Into this uncertain picture steps the band director. His is a most decisive role in the life of a potential instrumentalist.

How can the band director help at this point? The good director is constantly alert for possible future bandsmen, but he must have those with talent. How does he find them?

There are a number of ways. First the band director expects students with a sincere desire to play an instrument to identify themselves. He will give them every opportunity; in fact, he will take steps to find them in the student body. How?

He might conduct a survey. Or he might distribute a questionnaire at an assembly, in homerooms, or from the stage when his band plays a concert or assembly.

Desire and Interest

What does he seek first? He looks for those with a strong, obsessive desire to play an instrument. The student, of course, will need more than just desire to ensure a successful, happy band life. But without this hopeful beginning a director is at a loss, and a lukewarm, half-hearted interest at the outset generally leads to a very short-lived band life.

While desire is necessary, it is not necessarily talent, and it may not even indicate talent. Desire indicates interest, and that is a sound first step upon which to launch a fun-filled bandsman's life. Desire and interest, along with hope, are the right seedbed in which to begin.

There are two steps a hopeful band student may take at this point. The first one is to take a musical aptitude test. The second step is more practical in nature, and it is based on the grade the prospective bandsman makes on the aptitude test. The prospective bandsman should know the difference between talent and musical aptitude.

Measurements of Musical Aptitude

Musical talent cannot be measured, but the aptitude for musical achievement can be measured. A number of standard tests are available. The good ones will show a hopeful young musician how he ranks in his own musical potential or aptitude.

The term musical aptitude is in itself a generality. It includes certain specifics, however, such as particular areas of musical activity. They are: melodic, rhythmic, harmonic, tonal memory, timbre recognition, pitch discrimination, and tonal duration.

A good musical aptitude test measures each of these areas. The band director who administers the test can fully explain the meaning of these terms. The student should approach the aptitude test strongly determined to do his very best. Beginning bandsmen in school systems where such tests are yearly standards should know one important fact: the student's band career may very well rest on how well he does on this test.

A prospective bandsman is not ready to take practical steps to use his assumed talent until its presence has been confirmed or denied. This he will learn as a result of a good musical aptitude test.

Musical Aptitude Tests

The best all-round example of a good musical aptitude test is the Seashore. It has been a classic test for many years and is often used as a screening entry examination by music conservatories and professional music schools. It is comprehensive, covering all areas of musical hope or potential. It is also quite complicated for a very young student, and especially so for a student who has never faced such a test before. For this reason most high school band directors consider it too difficult for beginning band students.

The Tillson-Gretch Musical Aptitude Test is also comprehensive, but it is fairly easy for today's beginning bandsman to understand. In fact, it explains itself on two LP records. The test itself is taken on standard forms. The musical sounds come from the two records. Interested students may take the Tillson-Gretch test individually or in groups.

From the band director's viewpoint, group testing is to be desired. Grading may be done quickly and accurately by means of a card overlay. A corps of advanced band students can easily grade hundreds of these tests in less than an hour. The grading schedule is scored for students of different ages.

The Tillson-Gretch Musical Aptitude Test has been used to test students from third grade through twelfth grade in public school music programs. Under fair testing conditions, it is a reliable indicator of a person's musical capability.

Some major band-instrument manufacturers have developed other tests, ranging from the very good to the very simple. Some are too simple, in fact, to be sound or reliable. It is safe to say that the simpler the test is, the less reliable it is.

A band director armed with the results of a good M.A.T. (Musical Aptitude Test) is then ready to advise an impatient beginner. At this point both director and student have reached step two.

How to Find the Right Instrument

In this matter personal choice or desire is the first consideration. Beginning bandsmen usually know what they want to play, but with M.A.T. results as a guide, both student and director can see two things: (1) what he is strong in; and (2) his weak points. This information narrows the instrument list considerably. The test results will indicate probable difficulty, success, or failure on certain instruments.

The final selection of an instrument is the first practical step for the beginner. His choice should be guided by: (1) his own desire; (2) the M.A.T. results; and (3) the physical structure of the student's face, mouth, and teeth if his choice is a wind instrument. His physical size has some general bearing upon his ultimate choice. His height and arm length, even his physical strength, enter into the selection of the right instrument.

The band director launches a musical adventure early each school year: his beginner program. Parents of beginners need not make a great cash outlay. They usually want simple answers to what appear to be simple questions: does my son or daughter have musical talent, and can he or she play the piccolo, the flute, or the tuba?

Such questions can be answered in a matter of three or four months, which is the usual "rental-purchase" plan offered by nearly all band-instrument companies. The cost is nominal, often ten or fifteen dollars a month, which can usually be applied toward purchase of the instrument if it proves to be the one for the student.

The program is based on the simple yet sound adage, "Nothing ventured, nothing gained." Some students can and do succeed on their instruments "self-taught." But trial and error without competent instruction invites disappointment and disaster. Bad habits will invariably occur that will create major problems later.

Talent or Practice?

Once the student has selected his instrument, he enrolls in a beginner class. Here the director will recognize and build up the student's strong points. As for the student's musical weaknesses, if any, director and student must work together.

All musical work should be done with one ear on the strong points and the other on weaknesses, the goal being to balance the two. In the long run, then, the bandsman's weaknesses become passable or at least have been overcome to an acceptable point.

His strong points can make a spectacular and outstanding musician, and it will be precisely because his band instruction has built up his best capabilities as indicated on his M.A.T. His practical efforts at selecting the right instrument to fit his physical capabilities are most important, too.

No serious band student should ever think that he has so much talent that he need not practice. The old truism, "Practice makes perfect," should be plastered over his door. It wouldn't hurt to put it in his instrument case, too.

A great talent will fade away without practice. The driving need to practice is ever present. Practice must be regular. Talent, both large and small, is a raw force that must be formed and refined. Without practice, regular work, and structure, it remains forever a mass of raw energy. Talent alone will never produce a great clarinetist, trumpeter, or trombonist. Talent alone cannot develop skill. And skill is the name of the game in the high school band.

COURTESY *THE CREATIVE WORLD* OF STAN KENTON

These young bandsmen at Redlands University are off to a good start with the great Stan Kenton.

Using Your Talent

Talent is the road sign that points to a musical destination. But the road to skill is "practice highway." Talent without practice goes nowhere. The tortoise and the hare live herein. A mediocre talent may often be seen by the very talented as a tortoise. But with determination, drive, tenacity, self-discipline, and good practice habits, this tortoise will leave the lazy, ill-informed, and extremely talented hare far behind in his musical dust.

No matter how great or small one's talent may be, he has an obligation to it. He must do his best to mold a musical structure of it. The best way to do this is through practice. In rehearsals and performances, then, such talent development brings recognition. This, in time, leads to great personal satisfaction. What is a musician if he cannot play music that shows off his skill, feeling, expression, and technical ability?

Perfect and Relative Pitch

Perfect pitch is the rare ability to recognize instantly a given note when sounded. To players of certain instruments perfect pitch is priceless. The violinist, trombonist, cellist, or player of another instrument with variable pitch problems needs perfect pitch. Some players of these instruments, however, succeed without it by developing what is known as "good relative pitch."

There is one chief but important difference between perfect pitch and relative pitch. A person is born with perfect pitch; it cannot be developed later. But a good relative pitch can be developed. It must be fed, nursed, and used regularly and methodically; it requires constant attention; but good relative pitch is possible to achieve.

One must be born with the capacity or potential to develop good relative pitch, however. Here again, taking a good M.A.T. will indicate the potential bandsman's possibilities in this area.

The chief responsibility of perfect or relative pitch is to tell the player if he is in or out of tune. Many great musical stars have neither type. The numbers of vocal soloists who cannot sing in tune with an orchestra are legion. But bandsmen are not permitted this license. The good instrumentalist must develop good relative pitch, if he is not cursed or blessed with perfect pitch.

V

TRIAL BALLOONS

The Band Beginner

A beginner in band is very busy at first. He floats his "trial balloons." How so? His initial desire or impulse to try a particular instrument was a trial balloon. It may or may not have been shot down by his second trial balloon, the Musical Aptitude Test. His third floating effort should be his successful participation in the school band program.

The determined, dedicated student reaches the point where his balloons are sailing. Then he in capable of contributing. The questions arise: contribute what? And how? In what ways? To what or to whom?

The beginning bandsman contributes. But he does not know what or how or to whom. He is too concerned with himself. His own efforts are struggles with his own problems. This is as it should be. But after fair progress, the question of contribution arises and must be answered.

Contribute what? The answer is simple: contribute whatever skill and musicianship one has developed to date. His practice record so far is like a time investment. He has made an investment in his own talent, whatever it may prove to be. By contributing now what he has learned to do musically, he will begin to realize real interest on his musical investment.

How can one still at a beginner level contribute? By playing his best on his instrument in whatever group he finds himself. The good band student is more than a little competitive. He wants to sound better than others, to be able to play hard passages better than others in his group. He should contribute his technique, whatever it proves to be at that point.

Such a student can make very great contributions by listening to himself. He must hear his voice, not as a lone one, but as a part of others. He should hear the group and his own part within it. His ability to do so marks the beginning of real musicianship. His great contribution would be to add a good musical sound to the group effort.

Maximum Contribution

It should be noted that at no time is extreme loudness or maximum volume a maximum contribution. In fact, it would be the opposite. The best tonal contribution is only possible by soft-tone playing.

The alert bandsman soon becomes conscious of the full group sound. That is what audience and critics hear when he finally plays in a public performance. It would be better for everyone concerned if the student were well drilled on the quality of group sound.

How does the group or band class or section sound? The honest answer will depend on the honest combined efforts of all players. No amount of directing or conducting or baton-waving can do much to make pleasant a musical passage played by several bandsmen who are not really listening to themselves play.

Each player should listen to himself, but he must hear the others both individually and as part of the entire group. This is part of musicianship, but it is not all of it.

Some band students ask why must they try to do all this; such students should take up some other type of endeavor. A short stint on a mountain-climbing team would quickly reveal the need for maximum individual effort: it has to do with his own survival and that of his related group.

The situation is no different in band. The group, section,

class, or performing band will rise or fall on one ladder: the maximum musical contribution and effort of each individual student. With such effort the public esteem for the band can only rise.

Ways of Contributing

The high school bandsman's life is rich in opportunities. He would do well to go over the ways that he personally can contribute to a better band. In fact, the trained musical talent owes it to himself, his talent, his parents, his fellow bandsmen, his community, and lastly, to his director. He should compete to give the very best that is in him.

He should be attentive to all direction and instruction. He should contribute his full cooperation to his section-mates and to the full band or ensemble to produce the finest musical result. The bandsman impelled by desire, talent, and real imagination realizes the musical problems that can be solved only by practice.

This successful solution of musical problems is a definite contribution to the group effort. In fact, it may be the first and only solution. If so, everybody in the section and the band will benefit. This then becomes a student's major contribution.

The top bandsman is constantly alert for ways to help the band improve. A mediocre band is little better than no band. Who in his right mind would want to be a part of such a musical group? He who can join and measure up to high standards in a top band will be justly rewarded.

The good band director is ever trying to reward and recognize his real contributors and his top players. They are usually one and the same, but not always. There are exceptions.

Nonmusical Contribution

Often a minor or mediocre talent realizes his own limitations but earnestly wants to do everything possible to add or contribute to the band. There is a way open to such people: they may contribute through service.

Playing an instrument is the chief concern for musical contribution, to be sure. But there are many other areas of real need in a band.

A well-organized operating band is identical to any other operating public institutions. Every institution is made up of many small offices, duties, and services. Even a fine musical organization must concern itself with details.

When a band becomes so good that it arouses great community pride and esteem, the public looks upon it as an institution. And when that time comes, things change. The public makes demands of its institutions. But glorious is the band that basks in so great a reputation.

To maintain its status in institutional glory, however, some one must perform a thousand small duties and services. Who will do these things?

Many tasks can be assigned, but things done behind the scenes seldom get public recognition. This the wise director will correct on concert night. All contributors should be recognized, whatever their amount, type, or area of contribution.

2051452

How to Get Services and Duties Performed

Groups and individual students must share duty assignments. The well-organized band has or should have many small operational groups within its overall instrumentation. In some bands these work or duty groups may be called corps, in others, committees. The object is not to find the most impressive name. The real point is to organize the large band into many small groups. This smooths the path for the band to make its maximum impression on its concert audience when the time comes.

Many small details go into what appears to be an effortless performance on stage. A hundred or more small duties must be done. Who will do all this? Volunteers? A wise band director makes definite assignments to volunteers and daily follows up to see that things are moving along to the desired conclusion. If left entirely to volunteers, all too often things have a way of not getting done, and it is impossible to determine who is really at fault.

For this reason, it is wise to form duty corps or committees, to assign tasks, and to set deadlines.

The Feeling of Belonging

No band, not even a great high school band, is made up 100 percent of first-rate musical talent. Who composes the rest of its membership? And what level is the talent in question? In many cases a large portion of a band, or many of its members, are of average ability or even less.

Such students may take longer to perfect their parts on a composition being studied by the band. They may not grasp musical ideas as quickly as the more experienced members. But these same students are often strong on effort. They may be willing to spend more time than usually expected or required in practice. They will want to ensure their continued membership in the band. It is exciting and inspiring just to be a part of a fine band.

These weaker players realize their musical limitations. Some of them will try to improve their situation by performing services for the band or the director. In this way they feel more a part of the band and its musical work.

There is nothing wrong in this. Those who wish to serve should be allowed to do so. They should also be rewarded for their service or duty.

Whatever the goals of the high school band, it should reflect the entire school and community. Some directors, however, do not share this view. Some admit into the band only the super-talent, only students with IQ's of 110 or higher. Their players must be accomplished soloists and virtuosi. Such directors have no place in public schools.

Taxpayers have rights. Their children have a right to a chance at band. The total band experience is so rewarding that it is one of the school's enrichment programs. However, the band is an organization. It is a musical one, to be sure, but no organization can be made up only of chiefs; there must be some Indians to make the tribe go around. So it is with band.

Lesser talents may perform important services and duties. Many details must be accomplished before the band gets upon the concert stage or meets its public performance commitments.

In duty assignment corps or committees, social relationships are formed. Work is shared. Frequently these friendships would never have been made had it not been for the duty or service assignment. These details cut across sections and families of instruments. They are no respecters of grade level, physical size, or sex.

A great band can be no greater than its organization. If all needs, services, duties, and background works are well organized and under the director's firm control, the band is free to fly into musical orbit.

And that is the object of it all, is it not?

The playing and the hearing of thrilling music make it all worthwhile. The experience of making the music or helping to make it possible will never be forgotten.

VI

MAJOR REWARDS IN BAND

The Beginner's Outlook

Most beginning bandsmen take their chair with one strong, all-consuming, impatient urge. They want to make "instant music." All things are possible. But instant melody and musical skill may take a little longer.

But it is good that the impatient beginner should have this driving desire to make music *now*. Such an outlook is healthy. It indicates power drive, which will be needed later. Instant musicianship is unlikely, but such an obsession is the usual case.

Without a strong desire to make something musical, melodic, or rhythmic—and soon—the director and student both have an uncertain beginning at best. And this is exactly what neither wants.

A continual, gradual success in band depends greatly on a good solid beginning. The first-year player should not be dismayed by his earliest efforts. Most students experience similar things: sour notes, split tone, squawks, squeaks, or rasping sounds. Such students should tell themselves one thing: "Hang in there! The fun is just around the corner."

Questions Beginners Ask

The first question is likely to be, "What am I going to get out of all this?" The student who begins his band work with this question must do the following. He must write down what he wants from band. Then he must go over this list. He should be sure at this time also to write down how he plans to achieve each desire or expectation he lists. He must be sure to include what part he intends to play in reaching each goal or expectation.

Generally speaking, the student gets from band what he puts into it and more. Whatever reward he gets for putting himself into the total band effort will be but a small part of what he really will receive from his experience.

The average student will gain a great deal of inspiration and "soul food" from the efforts of his fellow bandsmen, but he may not realize this until after his beginner stage. Some time usually elapses before the bandsman becomes aware of the total group effort going on around him.

Another likely early question is, "How soon will I get my reward?" This can be answered by asking another question of equal significance: "How far is up?" Who knows when rewards will come, or even what rewards? The time when a band student begins to realize rewards depends on him, on his particular fellow bandsmen, on the director, on the amount of his home practice, and, of course, on the instrument he has selected for himself.

The matter of home practice is all-important. It may not always be a pleasant task, but its results eventually will be pleasant. Most people enjoy doing something they do well. Everyone likes success, and success leads to even more success. Rest assured, success in band depends on practice. The more the better. However, good practice habits are decisive when results are counted.

The student bandsman and the instrument he chooses are also important. For this reason, the beginner has a better chance of success by putting himself entirely in the director's hands. Very often the band beginner selects an instrument for which he is totally unsuited. Failure more than likely will be the unhappy result. The band director can help. He wants to help select the right instrument for each student. Why?

No band director wants to instruct a student on an instrument that clearly gives the beginner a hard time from the very outset. The wise student should choose that instrument on which it is easiest for him to produce a musical tone.

This solves the first problem facing all beginning bandsmen: tone production. Now and then a beginner chooses the impossible. He wants to play an instrument on which he can't even get a sound, to say nothing of a musical tone. Huff and puff though he may, nothing musical happens. In his case, several efforts at different times should be made. If still no tone is forthcoming, it would be wise to choose another instrument.

In any case it is well to remember: success makes a musician and failure makes a critic. The world has a surfeit of critics, but musicians are rare. They are a joy to hear, a blessing to mankind and bandkind alike.

In selecting an instrument, one should not stop with one or two. The beginner should try an instrument from each family of instruments in the band. If he is serious, persistent, and of great desire, he will eventually find the right instrument for him.

He will recognize "his" instrument when he tries one and easily produces a tone on it. The eternal hope is that the tone will be a relatively good one and not merely a noise. It is not for nothing that one horn was once called the "blatweasel."

Families of Instruments

Instruments are divided into families: (1) brasses, which include trumpet, cornet, trombone, baritone horn, bass horn or tuba, sousaphone, alto horn, altonium, and French horn; (2) woodwinds, including clarinet, saxophone, oboe, bassoon, flute, piccolo, alto and bass clarinet, and contra-alto and contra-bass clarinet; and (3) percussion, including snare drum, bass drum, xylophone, marimba, bells, chimes, kettledrums or tympani, and all other rhythm novelty instruments.

Musical Rewards

At this point intelligence enters the picture, if it has not already done so. It does not follow talent, choice of instrument, desire, or home practice. Intelligence should have been present throughout. The higher the student's intelligence, the greater his chances for success. But one should not be misled.

Everyone in the band, including the director, does not have genius-level intelligence. Bands, like school and society itself, are made up of average minds and players. Some bandsmen have extraordinary talent. Others work hard to become even average. But, as in band, so in life. An above-average band is the desired goal. A superior one is the ideal. In any case, for an introduction to life's circus, where everyone is on his trapeze or high wire doing his thing, one should join the band.

There are both obvious and hidden rewards for excellence. The challenge is to see how high one can fly on his instrument. The higher and faster the better. But this is figuratively speaking. The "pursuit of excellence" is the name of the game. The excellent or superior bandsman adds to the total excellence or superiority of his band.

The Paradox of Superiority

All band directors work hard to develop musical excellence or superiority in each student. The reason is painfully clear: it is a musical impossibility to build a superior band composed entirely of inferior players.

It is rewarding to play an instrument so well that listeners are visibly and emotionally moved. Favorable audience reaction is thrilling to the bandsman. This is a very personal and private reward; it proves that his efforts, hopes, and dreams were not all in vain.

A *Thrilling New Language*

It is commonly said that "Love is the universal language." Bandsmen of America, however, take note! Love is not the *only* universal language. Music is also a universal language. Beautiful

This drum major's "reward" was unexpected but one he seems to have enjoyed.

music, inspired melody, or rich, flashing harmonies can and do thrill listeners who cannot even communicate with each other because of language or handicap barriers. This kind of experience enriches the lives of millions.

But the bandsman reaps an even greater reward. Playing that gives pleasure to listeners thrills and enriches the player's life, too. Thus it is doubly rewarding. Such a bandsman will always be the richer for his experience. His musical work elevates his life forever. Music has changed his life for the better. Is this not a true and lasting reward?

Social Rewards

There is a great deal more to band than playing an instrument. To be sure, the music comes first, but it cannot stand alone. A band member belongs to a group or a team. Team feeling in band is just as important as team effort on the first-string football squad, if not more so.

The final overall image of the total band is what counts. A good musical effect is the chief objective of the band director, but it is not all. Let us not forget that an impressive band is made up of young people. To make a great performance, they must work hard together to reach that high goal.

Togetherness in the band world must never go out of style. The sense and sensation of individual bandsmen playing together thrills both players and audience. Never underestimate that. In-fighting among soloists or within sections creates a tense, ugly atmosphere. It does not add to the maximum beauty of performance. It shatters the band composure and disturbs the director. Worst of all, it destroys the band.

The Value of Competition

Keen competition between soloists vying for higher ranking chairs, however, is good. But only if it does not breed ugliness or ill-feeling. If it makes enemies instead of competing new or old friends, the band and director both have a problem.

There are true rewards in friendship. The beginning bandsman sees the problems of his new instrument. That is a musical problem. He may also have a social problem. Perhaps for the first time he is thrown into a "group effort." It may be an entirely new type of situation for him.

The first thing to do is to make friends. Then mistakes, sour notes, squawks, squeaks, or such problems become easy to deal with. Everyone in band is in it together. One may strengthen ties with old friends.

Each beginner certainly meets new people. He would do well to try to make new friends and not new enemies. By working

Togetherness is a "massed bands" show on the village green, especially if it's away from home on an overnight trip.

hard toward friendships, the student enriches his entire life.

He will be a better, happier bandsman and human being for his effort, and he will be rewarded with a host of new friends, all sharing a common aim: a superior band. This goal can never be realized by a roomful of enemies all trying to play louder and faster than everyone else.

Everyone wants to "belong." The outsider is to be pitied; he suffers, often alone and in silence. But the "outsider" in band can be a serious problem, affecting the band members and the director as well. Shared feelings and experiences mold a group together as nothing else can. Students then feel that they belong, and their productivity will increase in size, stature, and frequency.

This sense of belonging and sharing is a great reward in itself. Without band, many students in high school never experience such feelings. Their lives are poorer for the absence. Belonging and sharing make the bandsman more aware of his own worth and place in the scheme and team of things. If he gained nothing else from band, that in itself would be a major achievement.

VII

~~~~~~

THINK BAND

~~~~~~

A Positive Attitude

He who wants to lead must first learn to follow. Every good band has a number of leaders. Better organizations even have assistant leaders. But not everyone in band is a leader, at least, not at first.

Every band must have a large number of bandsmen who are followers. They are leaders-in-waiting, so to speak. With talent and proper practice, they should become leaders.

All chiefs and no Indians can make for a phenomenal band, but it may be a terrible organization. A good organization is absolutely necessary in a fine band. Each beginner, therefore, should realize at the outset that he is low man on the totem pole. Automatically he becomes an Indian or a follower of chiefs or leaders. But he does not do so blindly. He may have voluntarily joined four teams.

Teamwork in Band

A beginning bandsman with work and talent reaches an intermediate band level. Very often the school has a full-fledged intermediate band waiting for him. It may even be a performing band. Some of these are called cadet bands.

Students who have studied, practiced, and worked rise out of the beginner class. At that point, most students want to perform, and they should do so. Public performance has a way of inspiring students to practice harder than ever.

Regardless of ability level, every performing band runs on

teamwork. Some new bandsmen will be members of four teams, which are different but related. Everyone and everything in band is related, although some new bandsmen do not realize this.

A strong musical talent often finds a four-team part difficult. If so, he would be wise to accept the situation. Hard work and friendly cooperation will improve his lot. The challenge to move up through the ranks is great. Such a student could well compare his own case with a football team.

Not everyone who goes out for football in August makes the first team. Some less skilled and inexperienced players will be on the bench. They may be second- or third-team players, but they still await their chance to get in the game.

Even a football team has sections within itself; guards, tackles, backs, center, and ends, each either singly or in pairs is a unit within the team. Band is the same. The first team greeting the new bandsman is the full band, or the first team.

Within that large overall group, the second team is the particular family of instruments his instrument represents—brass, woodwind, or percussion.

Within that family a third team emerges. Does he play trumpet, trombone, clarinet, or saxophone? If so, that instrument is, in itself, a team. The trumpet section is a team, just as the guard section of a football team is a unit or team effort on the gridiron. The only difference is that one is a sport and the other an art. Otherwise they are alike in that their effort makes the team succeed.

The fourth team in a large section, such as trumpet or clarinet, is the position: third trumpet or third clarinet, second, or first. Even within that grouping a breakdown exists or emerges. Who will be declared or earn principal third chair or become first chair, third clarinet?

Talent and Strength

It all depends on the individual bandsman. He can view the team structure of band and become so discouraged that he fades away in a total decline. If so, his talent was not great enough to sustain him.

On the other hand, a strong talent may chafe at the bit. He may be impatient or even angry at the structural situation hemming him in. If he doesn't like it, he should practice and work hard to rise above his low-man-on-the-totem-pole spot. Faint heart ne'er won fair lady, nor first chair or solo in a top performing band.

Chair Challenging

There are a number of ways for a hard-working bandsman to climb the ladder to first chair trumpet, clarinet, trombone, or whatever. Chair challenging is one of these ways. This practice is common to many bands; in others it is unheard of. Although it is a good system theoretically, like everything else, it has its flaws and faults.

In chair challenging, usually the director selects a difficult passage from the music on the stand. He lets the two students involved each take a turn at playing it. The better man wins. Or the director may choose a technical etude or exercise and allow the challenger and the challenged player some time to practice the music before listening and judging.

In any case, the competition should remain friendly, however fierce it may tend to become. He who loses this time may well be the victor the next time around. The good thing about chair challenge is that there always is a next time. That fact should spur the loser on to make a greater effort with more practice. Practice is all-important in challenging. In both instances, the challenge situation has elevated the level of playing in that team or section area of the band.

The challenger has raised the level of playing for the contested chair by becoming better than the former chair-holder and winning over him. Even the loser has elevated the lower chair he must take, because surely he brings to it superior ability, having once been good enough to hold a higher chair.

Other Methods of Advancement

Some band directors do not favor the challenge system, and they may have good reasons for not relying on it. Some students fear and positively shrink from challenging, even if it is possible in their band. Even many students in a challenge band never challenge the chair-holder above them. Why?

Their reasons, for the most part, are personal. The student involved may be too shy or retiring, although he may be the superior player. The question is, does he deserve to gain the higher chair? It is not an easy question to answer in a band that uses the challenge system.

In a nonchallenge band, this situation is no problem. The director, recognizing the superior player, simply moves him up to the chair consistent with his talent and ability. This is a good system, provided the director is big enough to carry no grudges.

If he is fair in his student evaluations and placement, there is usually no trouble. If it arises, it may be quickly resolved by letting both students try the same test passage and decide who sits where.

The Bandsmen and the Director

The bandsman should consider at least two views of his own band situation, whatever it might be. Generally speaking, there are two responsibilities in a successful student-director relationship. Make no mistake, a successful relationship is a MUST for a good band. Each has a definite responsibility to the other.

The director, by virtue of age, experience, and background, is or should be fairly well equipped to handle his end of the bargain. But the student is a growing organism, and a musical one at that. Everything does not come easily to one in transit— or to the advanced student, for that matter.

The good bandsman should recognize first his place on a team. It is a great musical team made up of smaller, inner teams.

At the top of that musical heap is one master: the band director. The student's part is to follow the director's leadership. The director's part is to lead in all phases of the band experience.

As long as both parties to the unwritten contract understand their part in band affairs, there is little trouble or friction.

Problems often arise with students, however. They forget their responsibility or position: theirs to play, and the director's to lead, instruct, counsel, and befriend until each player is eventually rewarded with success.

Rewards of Musicianship

Rewards for musicianship usually come only as a result of work, practice, talent development, and skill. A bandsman moves up the ladder from third chair to second to first to solo. His progress depends on talent, practice, and performance.

Honors, awards, and public recognition usually come to the skilled musical technician. The outstanding soloist in concert or at graduation seldom fails to receive both public acclaim and lasting mementos from the band or director. The John Philip Sousa Award, the Arion Award, and a Director's award go to the bandsman who works, plays, and gives of his talent to his band. They are prized and much coveted reminders of his days in his high school band.

Conduct Rewards

The new bandsman should accept the fact that good conduct improves his chances for fast advancement in the band. Alertness in following directions also is important. It would be foolish and unfair for a director to promote a bad actor even if he plays like a master. Devilish behavior should detain advancement. Lack of concern for one's teammates can and usually does destroy the desired effect. It restricts band progress and growth. Bad behavior should be counseled but never rewarded. To elevate a bad actor who plays well compounds the band's problems.

Bad attitudes must be faced head-on, and efforts made to resolve the problem. But in no case should the student involved be elevated to a more desirable chair so as to get rid of conflict.

Relationships with the Student Body

The good band student is a goodwill ambassador for his band, or should be. His immediate focus should be on the students he meets daily in class or elsewhere on the school grounds. It does not help the band to publicize its problems among nonmembers. It destroys the desired image. It rots the seedbed of potential band members. It disturbs parents who might be seriously considering their child's entry into the band program.

It gives the band a bad name. It limits the invitations for trips and performances away from the school. Band students should pursue good relations and a good image; it will pay them handsomely to do so.

Faculty Members

Everyone is proud of a winning team, be it football, basketball, or band. Faculty members are no exception. They want to think their school band is a fine musical organization, and bandsmen should never let them down.

The student who would honestly and fairly serve his band should never fail to point up its good features. Every band has good points; some bands have many. Seek out the strong points of the band, or discuss the matter with the director.

Band Booster Club

This is the next line of defense for the team-playing bandsman. Most advanced bands in schools with traditional band programs usually have a band booster club. Regardless of its name, it has one chief purpose: the care and aid of its band, whatever the needs may be.

Here again, the goodwill ambassador bandsman should work with these people. They have joined to help him and his band, their band. Only by working together can both bodies reach success in their joint endeavors.

The tendency of some parents and bandsmen to quarrel or find fault with every idea that comes up should be discarded. Getting along, having good relationships with everyone is the name of this particular game.

Civic Groups

In a widening circle beyond the band booster club, the bandsman becomes increasingly aware of civic groups. He may have lived in one community all his life yet never have really noticed a fact of life there.

His town or area is made up of many interlocking groups, the Civitans, the Ruritans, the Lions, the Rotary, the Chamber of Commerce, Shriners, VFW, the American Legion, or the Ladies Garden Society.

The good-will-minded bandsman must support these organizations too. Usually they are approached for contributions for band expenses or events. Their amount of interest and contribution in dollars and cents is directly related to the good relations existing between band and community. Individual band students relate. The entire band relates. The atmosphere must be friendly and cooperative.

Bandsmen in smaller communities would remember with profit: if they do not spend locally, can they expect local civic groups to spend funds on the local band? This is a key question in band finance.

VIII

BANDS AND MORE BANDS

The Standard Instrumental Music Program

The grade level of beginning band varies in different school systems. In some, band commences with fifth or sixth grade. In other schools, it may be offered to fourth- or even third-grade students.

In secondary schools it usually is offered to seventh- and eighth-grade students. Some four-year high schools may even have a beginning class in ninth grade. But regardless of grade level, beginning band class is vital. Without beginners there would be neither intermediate nor advanced band.

Often intermediate band is bypassed or does not exist. In a limited school situation there may be only beginner and advanced band levels. This is not ideal, but it is better than no band at all in the district.

The importance of numbers in the beginner band class is great. In order for a band to grow in size, quality, and repute, it cannot rely on a small yearly beginner class. The success, pride, esprit de corps, and public regard of a fine band are tied to size. A small band wherein each member is a superior player would be ideal to hear; but unless its sections are full as required in standard band arrangements, it is not a full, real band. Furthermore, such an exclusive band does not represent the entire musical or school community. Nor does it represent the entire civic community, the source of its financial support, regardless of size.

A large yearly beginner class is essential to resolve the real problem of building and maintaining a fine, full band of any symphonic proportions of instrumentation. That problem is getting people into the band program and keeping them there until they grow into superior players. Then they are available to replace departing and graduating band members. It is a kind of

Good student directors may begin at any level.

insurance that a good, standard symphonic balance can be met and kept.

Thus, numbers become a game. The far-seeing director must start great numbers in his beginner classes. He will lose students along the way. Some move out of town or go into other interests. Some develop school schedule conflicts. Others leave band by choice or personal necessity. A few are squeezed out by post-school goals that exclude their remaining in band.

Whatever the reasons, the band loses many potential members between the first year and last year of high school. A talented beginner class may start in fifth grade. Before entry into performing band, that group may lose 50 to 70 percent of its members.

Thus, all students who make satisfactory scores on musical aptitude tests must be attracted into beginning band. The natural process of selectivity, choice, maturing talent, or growing or waning interest will thin out the ranks.

This leads to a natural screening process. If a beginner class is large, when it reaches performing band level, enough students will remain to make director selectivity possible.

Intermediate Band

In schools with small total student enrollment and small performing bands, intermediate band may prove to be a luxury. The small school system will have a beginner band class that places students directly in performing or advanced band. This system without a middle group has one grave flaw.

All students from beginner class are eligible to go on into advanced band if they pass the course, but they may not all be good players. Some will be weak, bad, or borderline. In any given group there will be a range of abilities.

If all students pour out into performing band, the performance level necessarily goes down. The quality of band sound is not the most desirable. A serious problem now exists.

But, as with all problems, there are solutions. The weaker students may enter on a probationary basis, being required to remove deficiencies by a given deadline. The first semester is a good probation time.

Naturally, these weak players must fill lower-ranking section chairs. Although all positions and chairs are harmonically important in a band with a good overall sound, the first-chair players and soloists are the superstars.

Advanced Band

This is the standard combined band. When the band student reaches high school he suddenly finds himself in a swirl of activity. His band is now really two bands in one: marching and concert. Their combined yearly activities put his head in a whirl.

But the advancing bandsman likes this. At last he has reached a level where band means something publicly. He is doing something now with all those years of playing, study, and lonely practice he has done.

The new bandsman in a high school performing band has, in a sense, and often in his own young eyes, hit the big time. Performing band opens every school year as a marching unit. Has the new bandsman marched before? Many have not. Middle schools tend to deemphasize marching band, and in many it is never mentioned. Directors in junior high prefer to concentrate on musical development, tone, technique, and general musicianship. This is good.

But the high school directors their schools feed would like the incoming bandsman to have had some marching. No bandsman can join marching band in ninth or tenth grade and make any significant contribution unless he has had previous marching experience.

Marching while playing is something new and different. Some students have a hard time adjusting. Some cannot, whereas others take to it at once. Players become stronger and contribute more as their experience in marching band grows. In the second or third year of marching and playing the student begins to show great playing power while on the march. This is what the director has been waiting for during the bandsman's entire membership in the marching unit.

The standard high school performing band is as advanced as its weakest players allow. Lack of precision, both in playing and marching, disillusions every audience. Yet that very band may have many fine players. People tend to notice mistakes, however, the visible lack of precision and human error in the marching band.

In concert, the sour notes, bad tones, and overall lack of ability of weak players hit the audience's ear first, last, and always. This predetermines their opinion of the full band. Thus,

Filling the street with uniformed musicians and solid marching music is the band director's goal on parades.

the bad players appear to have more audience impact than good ones.

The combined marching-concert band offers its members variety of activity from week to week. Some directors think the combination band also has many built-in problems. It may have, but it all depends on how one looks at problems. Usually they can be turned into opportunities.

The problem most directors see in a combined band is that the marching band carries over too far into concert preparation season. The usual demands made by school and community on marching band keep a bandsman jumping. Most band students like this. They enjoy the activity and the change, and well they might. It is the time of their lives.

Directors, however, have a slightly different view. The pressure of concert and festival competition commitments weighs heavily on them. Often the marching band instrumentation varies when the band moves from gridiron into concert season. Some students double on a different concert instrument.

This instrumental changeover takes time. Several weeks are necessary before a fair concert sound emerges. Street or gridiron sound and concert sound are not the same. Directors would like them to be identical, but this is impossible. The concert stage demands rigorous attention to perfection of tonal quality, accuracy of technical passages, and good volume or dynamics control and expression.

But, in this case, directors should take heart. A band that has had varied demands made on it by the community is in a good bargaining position when it needs financial help from the community. Every band has many needs; financial ones are among the greatest.

Therefore, the pressures of an overdemanding public can be turned into a positive situation, giving the director and band an opportunity later to ask for and expect financial help.

Orchestra

Many good school systems do not have a string or orchestral program, but all schools should. In some areas this may seem impossible. In others, the cost overshadows community support and interest.

Strings and orchestra are a must for a first-rate, well-developed instrumental music program. This area requires an accomplished string instructor for success. A makeshift director will have a makeshift orchestra.

Extracurricular Instrumental Groups: Stage Band

Many school systems, both large and small, have not yet realized that stage band is here to stay. It has long since become respectable in progressive areas, however. In many traditional schools, stage band may meet after school or even in the early morning before school. In such schools, administrators exhibit little interest in this area of the instrumental music program, which is unfortunate for the young people involved.

In these situations, the school administrators do not regard stage band highly enough to offer it for credit as a curriculum class. It is up to the director, the students, and the parents, if necessary, to force the issue. Stage band is a rapidly expanding and developing student-oriented subject. It merits classroom study and credit along with English, shop, or math. In many cases, stage band is a practical apprenticeship for students who leap from high school into income-producing music groups. Thus, it is on-the-job training. As such, it should not be ignored by administrative policy and decision makers.

Ensemble

Most schools exist within a framework of regional and state solo and ensemble or concert band competition festivals. Yet few schools offer solo and ensemble as a credit class. Here again, although the pressure is on a band to produce meritorious ensembles for state competition, no provision is made for their accredited organization or development as a curriculum offering.

In fact, it is fashionable to leave all that up to the director. When he develops these ensembles is up to him, but it must be done before school, after school, or on weekends. If ensemble is worth having and competition in the festivals is required, then it is worth including in the school curriculum. It should be a credit class meeting daily like all other regular academic subjects.

Jazz/Rock Ensemble

This type of band unit is on the rise dramatically. It should also be in the curriculum. Its literature is developing at an astonishing rate. Music for this group is much more rhythmic than melodic, yet it receives wildly enthusiastic response from the student body in assembly. It is most popular with bandsmen and other students.

IX

ORGANIZATION OF BAND

Standard Band

Standard bands are made up of sections, instrumental groups that are the superstructure of any band. Within the larger, complete family voices of brass, woodwind, and percussion, the band has smaller units, the sections: trumpets, trombones, clarinets, saxophones, flutes, baritone horns, tubas, and French horns.

The large overall family units are often called "sections" too, which may be confusing. Students in band may have trumpet sectional rehearsals one day and brass sectionals another. New students soon learn the difference.

Other smaller subsections exist within the proper section. In the trumpet section, one finds first trumpet, second, and third. Each of these groups is a unit, calling for players to play a different musical part from the other two.

All these units, subunits, and family groups constitute the standard band. They are its strength and its structure. Without these units playing together on different parts at the same time, the band sound would be something entirely different.

Full Band

The full band is the great concern. The listening audience hears the combined sound of all sections, subsections, and families of instruments playing together. But bandsmen hear things differently. Members of a performing band have grown musically.

They should be able to hear each family and section. The better players should even hear the subsections. Good players should be able to hear the subsection members of their own section, at least. Such hearing ability, or musicianship, is necessary for the finest sectional balance and musical nuance.

Band Officers

Positions of responsibility and honor in a fine band are based on merit and not on popularity. In standard bands a common organization built on merit and musicianship would have a structure like the following:

At the top and next to the director are assistant or student-assistant conductors. Next in rank are the sectional soloists, section leaders, and assistant section leaders. An advanced band with considerable concert background may have a concertmaster. This is usually the first oboist or first clarinetist, to whom the band tunes in the absence of electronic tuner.

Marching band may have a drum major, drill-masters, assistant drillmasters, and rank and file or squad leaders. These students correct and help train new marching band members. They assist the director in precision marching efforts and maneuvers.

Formal or Military Band

In the band organized along strictly military lines, the bandsman rises through the ranks. Echelon and grade are important words here. As a new student, one may enter band as a third-class bandsman. The means of rising in the ranks may rest upon a musical exam of practical playing, theory, and drill. Success promotes one from third class to second, first, section leader, soloist, and then at last, student-assistant conductor.

Merit and Service

The military-style band organization may have rank or positions based on service. These positions are earned by members who perform a definite and important service, which may not relate to musical performance at all.

The head librarian, sectional librarian, instrument and equipment repairer, drillmaster, squad leader, stage manager, and photographer are such positions.

These bandsmen have worked hard and earned their rank in a military-style band.

Titles and Recognition

In the military type of band, each position has a rank and corresponding stripe, bar, or other visual ornament that designates quickly his chair, position, or office.

The lowest or entry-level rank is Third Class Musician or Bandsman. This seat merits one stripe, if chevrons are the designating ornament. Second Class wears two stripes, and First Class wears three. Assistant section leaders wear three stripes up and one down, section leaders wear three up and two down. Soloists merit three up and three down, and assistant or student conductors may wear three up, three down, and a diamond in the center.

Styles change in these sleeve chevrons. Different designations or designs can always be adapted to the particular level or situation.

Then, too, West Point stripes may be used. These have accompanying officer titles and are slightly different than the noncommissioned rank chevrons mentioned earlier.

In some situations in a military-style band, a student may pass a test for a higher chair. He may be awarded the stripes to befit his new rank and chair, but he may have to remain where he was in the section in order to maintain the proper tonal balance. In this case, at the first vacancy, or if a higher-chair student slips in his work, this student rises to the chair of his newly earned rank.

There are, however, certain problems of change in the highly militarized band. The first one is one of cost. These rank stripes cost money. The West Point stripes in particular are quite expensive. A large band, once it has a full set of stripes, incurs little expense thereafter, but the initial cost runs into several hundred dollars.

Problems of change arise when students lose rank. Many do not want to give up their hard-earned stripes, or those who move away "forget" to return their stripes with their uniforms. This increases operating costs.

The Case Against Challenging in Military-Style Band

Challenging definitely presents problems, but it should be mentioned in discussing military band structure. In the typical challenge, the two students involved play for an exchange or defense of position or chair. The director's decision is based on a numerical or quality comparison of one musical passage played on the spot. It may even be done after school with only the director and the two players present. But to make important changes in chaired personnel just before a concert or public performance is disastrous. It is extremely damaging to the band's overall musical effort and sound.

The student who loses out may be more capable in other important musical areas of technique, expression, control, or in home practice. He may contribute much more in many areas than an opponent. His cooperation may be twofold that of the successful challenger.

It is, therefore, extremely unfair to unseat him on the basis of one chance trial-and-error passage and give his much-deserved chair to another. The successful challenger may have made fewer mistakes, yet he may never contribute in other areas of band work.

There are arguments for chair, rank, and file exams. Here the bandsman competes with himself, facing a standard in order to elevate his chair or position. If he passes the requirements, both in music and service, he takes the standard test for the higher chair and is graded accordingly. Thus, he wins or loses a new or more desirable rank. But his win or loss depends on much more than a two- or three-minute playing exhibition.

Satisfactory service, attitude, and time in grade or chair are very important factors in a student's receiving promotion.

There are many hidden factors related to first-chair position. The better the band, the better the player and the more is involved in his position. It is, therefore, imprudent to elevate a third-chair or second-chair player to first or soloist based on a two-minute challenge situation.

It is extremely unfair to the student who loses. It is also unfair to the whole concept of band. Playing the instrument is first and foremost, to be sure. And band means playing the instrument as well as possible at all times. But everyone makes mistakes. To lose a position of honor because a director is counting the mistakes of two competitors is organizationally unsound.

Chair challenge could be more fairly used if the total records of both students involved were studied and evaluated. This process can be used in bands of military structure and style. A second-chair trumpet player may become lazy. He may not practice. He falls down on his total contribution. He shows no evidence of technical progress. He apparently is not trying for first chair. He may very fairly lose out to a hard-working third-chair player.

Especially is this true if the third player wishes advancement, if he works hard for it and passes the second-chair test with flying colors. In this situation a challenge is in effect, but its result is not based on a brief passage, with the director counting the mistakes like a football referee. The challenge is in effect all the time when chair or rank tests are the order of the organization.

Performing Groups Within the Band: Formal Ensembles

In all bands, both standard and military, the band students enjoy smaller playing groups. The formal, competitive ensembles, that is, brass, woodwind, percussion, or mixed winds, produce better players. The better the band, the better its ensembles.

These festival competition ensembles are musically rewarding to the members. They are memorable experiences, especially for those who win the honors.

Such ensembles must be formed, however, on a basis of technical equality rather than on friendship. In a winning combination ensemble, the student makes new friends. Regardless of competition results, however, the experience is beneficial and memorable. It points up strengths and weaknesses.

The festival winners always receive medals, certificates, and publicity. This always increases the student's esteem and acceptance among his peers. His obvious musicianship increases his self-esteem and self-confidence.

Fun Ensembles

In this area fall rock, jazz, and jazz/rock, the new and widely popular small groups within the big band itself. Most bandsmen want to participate in one of these units, but not all instruments have parts written into such arrangements.

The big band that has one or more jazz/rock combos within its overall membership enjoys wide acceptance by the student body and even the outside community. It adds variety and spice to the band concert when that band performs.

Pops concerts have become the "in" thing. Groups performing this kind of program can well use the repertoire provided for stage band or jazz/rock ensemble. The students who play in these fun ensembles reap a side-effect reward: it speeds up their technical ability even for symphonic and concert music performance. These players swiftly become the best players in the larger concert or symphonic band. They also become the envy of other bandsmen and the rage of the student body.

As another fringe benefit, these ensembles and their performer-members receive more requests to play dances, proms, weddings, and other affairs than they can fill. The chance to earn money from their music has arrived. Professionalism is either near or just around the corner.

Pep Bands

These should be volunteer groups, with the director keeping an eye on the membership. The pep band should be fairly well balanced sectionally. Numbers should be kept small. Pep bands play mostly in the gym, at rallies, or in the school auditorium. They are asked to play at basketball games. In these places the full sound of the large band is undesirable. Gym echoes are monstrous and unmusical.

By using a small group, however, the amount of echo is greatly reduced. A crowded gym during a basketball game also has little space to give to a one-hundred piece band.

X

REALIZING RELATIONSHIPS

Kinds of Directors

The good band director has recognizable qualities. His personality often defies analysis. In the first place, fine directors are made, not born. Such men are developed by experience; the demands of their work have shaped them.

All directors, however, should have certain general qualities. Fine musicianship, a good musical ear, skill, and training are first. A good director must have a sense of fair play. He must be able to make quick, fair judgments. He must be a strict disciplinarian if need be.

He must be a drill instructor, father-confessor, or slave driver at times. He may have to crack the whip, be a warden, or a snake-charmer. Among the first requirements are his sense and skill in diplomacy. In order for the band to exist and progress, he must be a press agent and fund-raiser.

For all these reasons, band students often misjudge their band director. The student may see only one side of him—the one the bandsman does not like or doesn't want to see. This is particularly true when it comes to discipline.

But a good director can be friendly, too, if allowed to be so. It would be wise for the student to remember that the director has at least four major facets. The question of whether he is fine or poor rests upon: (1) musicianship; (2) personal qualities; (3) duty demands; and (4) grace under pressure.

A fine director is expected to excel in certain musical areas. They are: musicianship, conducting, judgment, placement of students, score reading, and musical expression.

BILL MINOR PHOTO

Even during a parade a director is listening to his band and making mental notes.

The director's personal qualities may make him well liked, but that which makes a fine musician often will not make him well liked. Hence, students and public alike must often forgo something in order to get an acceptable musical director. Put simply, a fine musical director is not always the most likeable. He is not necessarily a "good guy." Should he try to be?

He needs to be liked. But liking is somehow dependent on respect. If students and parents do not respect their director, they will not like him to be their director. There is a fine line of distinction. What they like in their director is more to the point.

69

A director's duties often require of him the image of the "tough disciplinarian." As such, he may often appear angry or unlikeable. Students should remember, however, that if the band is to be meritorious the director is the key. Without a good director, bandsmen will have little they later consider memorable in their band experience.

On the opposite side of the coin, a poor director can ruin a fine band. This is rare, but it is possible. The quality of a director rests on the depth and breadth of his musicianship, judgment, judicial taste, discipline, diplomacy, fund-raising ability, bookkeeping, and public relations.

If he is poor in a majority of his duty areas, he will fail to impress favorably. With such result, he will reap little friendship from either students or audiences.

The scope of the profession of band-directing demands the best and the most of men. The director must try to measure up to the demands of the field. The same is true of students, of course. The fault of many failing bands does not lie entirely at the director's door.

Kinds of Students

The first and foremost desirable quality of the good bandsman is identical to that of the good director. He should exhibit good musicianship qualities. These are the seedbed for success, honors, awards, and happy lifelong memories of days in the high school band.

Musically the bandsman must have some talent and capacity to perform. He must be willing to practice when his friends are trying to lure him off to recreation. He must be willing to give up things or to sacrifice free fun time to try to perfect his instrumental skills. The development of talent does not come automatically with time.

The good bandsman must be willing to work. He should have the capacity to discipline himself in order to improve technically. He should be social. He must be able to get along peacefully with director, fellow bandsmen, and competitive members of his section.

The good bandsman should be neat, trim, and personable. Marching band almost demands this. Bands of trim, neat students usually sound trim and neat. Good bandsmen should be friendly, but not too much so. They should be open and receptive to all directions from the director.

There are some common qualities of the good band student. They are quickly noticeable by director and more experienced bandsmen as well.

A weak player will argue and find fault with everything and everyone. He loudly proclaims his dislike of each musical selection unless he chooses it. Conditions on the field disgust him. The bus, or the principal, or his own instrument are blamed for problems he himself creates. Everything is troublesome. He is nearly always a very loud and vocal critic. This serves to hide the real truth.

He usually is either deliberately not playing well or cannot play well. He doesn't practice as he should. He wants to "get even" with the director for some imagined slight or disciplinary conflict. The bad bandsman must be eliminated at once. Given half a chance, he will ruin a good band.

In contrast, the good band student is guilty of none of these negative qualities. He is the opposite.

The Bandsman and His Fellow Bandsmen

There are but two general demands on the bandsman: musical and social. The normal musical demands should prove interesting and challenging. Often the bandsman may consider music uninteresting because he does not like the composition being played. If this is true, he should listen to the band more closely. He should remember that if he can play one hard passage that he doesn't like, later he will be more capable of playing one he does like.

Often musical demands seem too great for a particular student. This may indicate an extremely weak talent; it certainly indicates disinterest or faint heart.

The good player always likes a challenge. Difficult passages spur him on to greater efforts in his home practice. Good players always like to impress others.

A good bleacher band can make "close friendships."

Musical demands are made on the whole band, the section, and the subsection. The individual player must try to measure up to the level of the group or exceed it if possible.

As for social demands in a high school band, they are at every turn. The student must rub elbows with everyone in the band. He should avoid conflict as much as possible. The successful, happy, achieving bandsman must also prove himself a social animal. He must be able to get along with the full band and all its individual members.

Two counter-expectations are important in high school band. The student has expectations: what does he want from band? And what does the director expect or want from his students? If these two expectations are not identical, they should at least be similar. Both student and director should want progressing musicianship. This requires sincere effort and practice. The director expects loyalty to the band. Both director and student should expect work, concentration, practice, goodwill, and good humor at rehearsals. There should be a mutual will to work hard for mutual goals.

Goals

Early in his band career each bandsman must begin to think of goals. What are worthwhile goals for himself and his band? His musical ones come first; from them come all others. The bandsman should aim high. He can expect to work hard but gain greatly from his labors. His immediate world is going to concern himself, his musical associates, and his director.

The student should also set social goals and make honest efforts to realize them. He must adapt to others. It is essential that he get along with his fellow bandsmen. He should insist on making the social most of his high school band days.

The intelligent bandsman will have personal goals. Often bandsmen are too self-conscious to mention these to a director. One may dream of becoming a professional musician, of playing in a symphony orchestra or a popular performing-recording group. Each student should keep in mind his future goals with his daily ones.

Section goals are usually specific. Will the section play a difficult passage satisfactorily? Is there a deadline? Will the section sound well when it should? Can it execute the expression demanded in precise music? No group or section can achieve more than its individual members can produce together.

Full band goals are outlined and presented to the band by the director. They will be either social or musical, or a combination. The subject of democracy may enter in some cases; frequently, however, democracy in high school band has disappointing results.

A very democratic band may not be worth hearing when it plays. Some issues in band can be settled through the democratic process, but the band that votes on everything invites musical disaster—and usually receives it.

In certain situations the band may be democratic. But what, really, is democratic music? Or even music democratically played? More important, what does the supportive community want of its band: democracy or band? Each of these two subjects may be of great concern to the student today. But logically, the band most concerned with democracy will be perhaps least concerned with its music.

Practical Diplomacy

What should bandsmen do to get along well with others? The answer is: be sensible. Follow the golden rule: do unto others as you would have them do unto you. When conflicts arise, give and take. One cannot have all his wants. In the necessary close working relationships in band, one should beware of conflict. It can ruin a fine band in the making.

But how does one avoid conflict? Most conflicts arise as social problems, but most such problems in band stem from musical conditions. A bad or weak player turns into a social problem. His misbehavior is used to cover up the real truth: he can't play as well as he should or as well as others around him.

The director is the one to solve such problems. Good bandsmen must be intelligent enough to see through such sham. Instead of feeding disappointment and conflict, the wise bandsman should turn it over to the director.

XI

~~~~~~

TRIPS AND OTHER MUSICAL ADVENTURES

~~~~~~

Local Musical Events: Official and School-Related

Festival competitions occur yearly. The high school bandsman may want to participate in several types of these competitions. They include solo, ensemble, concert-band, stage-band, and jazz-band festivals.

Solo competition may suit the student who enjoys hard work alone. Such a student can find a long list of solo competitions available for his selection.

A good director will work with his students who prefer solo competition. Most band students, however, would much rather enter the full concert-band festivals. They feel stronger in the large group.

All grades and kinds of solo and ensemble music are available. Concert music is graded from I upward. All combinations of wind instruments are well covered by the standard literature. Ensemble practice and participation speed individual ability and progress and make the player alert to his immediate musical surroundings. His musicianship increases much faster than that of the noncompeting band member.

An ensemble should be organized for festival competition according to the ability level of its members. Popularity or close friendship should not be the concern. All ensemble members, however, must work and play together without friction.

Concert-band festivals are held in every state. In each case there is a statewide festival music list, arranged according to difficulty. Titles may vary, however. A selection may be grade III in one state and II in another or even IV in a third.

In any case, the director has an early annual goal before him. He must select good festival music to fit his players. It should offer a challenge, yet be capable of successful rendition. Will the players be able to execute it with such style that they can earn the high rating they all want? Selectivity is crucial to success. The composition should fit the organization.

It is almost impossible to win top honors in regional or state band festivals without a regular sectional rehearsal schedule. Students should expect and even want hours of extra rehearsal and practice. If sectionals cannot be scheduled during school hours, they must be done before or after school.

Honors and top grades scored by bands in regional and state festivals are tied to practice and more practice.

Stage-Band Festivals

Stage band is a more recent addition to regional and state festivals. These groups as traditional musical organizations are not officially recognized in some states. The more progressive locales, however, are instituting regular competitive programs, if they have not already done so. Some states have under way well-defined programs of festival activity for stage band.

The competition is full of jazz, rock, rhythm, and improvisation. It is wide open for instrumental combinations other than the traditional trumpet, trombone, drums, and saxophone. In some winning bands, flutes, bassoons, and French horns are orchestrated along with the usual instruments.

Stage band is the newest element of high school band festival competition. It is growing by leaps and bounds everywhere. Student interest is so high that competition is keen.

As a subject in instrumental music, stage band deserves its rightful place. It is not a lower form of musical life. Students are so interested in it in most places that stage bands will practice long after everyone else has gone home for the day. Players tend to develop a very high level of ability on their instruments. They add luster and brilliance to the concert bands of which they are members. For this reason, stage band should not go unrecognized. In schools where a fine concert or symphonic

BILL MINOR PHOTO

A parade out of town is a fun outing after the money for the trip has been earned.

band has long been the tradition, stage band should also be offered.

Athletics always occupies an extremely high position among student and community interests. Many athletic activities involve a band of some sort.

Football season requires a marching band to put on half-time and pregame shows. Smart coaches try to win the friendly cooperation of their fellow teacher, the band director.

77

In some communities the band is so highly regarded that it receives a part of the football gate receipts. This is highly desirable as a stable source of finance for band needs. One of the most important of these needs, as far as the band members are concerned, is to pay for trips. Some popular bands receive 10 percent or 5 percent of the gate at home football games.

Pep-Band Travels

In some areas, the full marching-concert band does not travel to away-from-home games. For these, pep bands are formed. Their cost is usually minimal, because such small numbers may go in private cars.

Pep bands are common at basketball games. Members should be the older and more experienced players from concert and marching band. A good balance should be maintained, rules and regulations should be established, and a student conductor should be appointed and trained. Many such performances must be made without the services of the band director. The purpose of mentioning pep bands here is to relate them to stage bands. Whereas the earlier, traditional assortment of bandsmen playing together as a "pep band" was acceptable, of late the stage band, where it exists, has come to be the unit that performs these functions.

A regular-instrumentation, full stage band requires its own library and has other expenses as well. Therefore, it cannot use the standard football music, and its cost may in part be paid from the percentage of the football gate, if the band receives one.

If the band is already enjoying this gate-receipt share, it is to be commended. Some enterprising, hard-driving, and successful band director put his neck on the block to accomplish that feat. If bands do not get a share of the football gate receipts, such bands, their directors, and their band booster clubs might profit by moving in that direction.

Local Concert Travel

The opportunities for local trips involving formal concerts are at hand. Schools within a given school district or the same county or region may arrange exchange concert programs. This travel can best be done during the school day. The concert band travels on a given day to a neighboring school, where they play an assembly concert. On a later date, the host school of that program sends its own band to play an exchange concert for the first performing band.

These exchange programs serve many good purposes. In the first place, bands get to hear one another. They can compare and learn to evaluate their own work better. The individuals become more aware that they do not exist in an academic or a musical vacuum. Others experience similar events, problems, and joys that go with the high school band. The students in the two bands concerned learn to see and hear good points along with the bad or the weak ones, increasing their overall musical knowledgeability.

Even the student audiences of the two bands become more appreciative. They, too, learn to compare and make musical evaluations. And the bands concerned get a day off from the regular school schedule now and then to break what may be academic monotony.

In some exchange areas, this program is well-established. The bands in such locales, as a result, are advanced, superior, and highly regarded by student bodies and parents as well. Being in band in such places has become important. In order for such exchange programs to be of any extent and to have greater comparability, seven or eight schools may be involved.

In such a program each band goes to a different school at least once a month during the school year, and their own student body gets to hear another different guest band at least once a month. All this activity in the music world calls attention to the full band and to each individual band member as well. This kind of public attention builds self-confidence, pride, and esprit de corps. A band that travels considerably soon becomes a closely knit organization.

Another important advantage of exchange concerts is that the bands get to hear considerably more music each school year. The home band can study only so much music each year. But if seven or eight bands come to their own school to perform different programs, the music they have heard and become familiar with is increased by as many schools as are concerned.

Competition between bands in these area-exchange concert programs is high. Individual bands strive to outplay and outwork all the bands they expect to hear that year. From the director's standpoint, these exchanges provide yet another service. In some cases, visiting bands have more complete symphonic instrumentation than the home band. The guest band may have instruments the director has been trying vainly to get financial support to buy. If his band and the student body sees a band with those instruments, word gets around. People want to appear progressive if financially able. It becomes easier to find funds to buy an instrument that most of the visiting bands already have.

Regional Collegiate Football Games

In many areas, colleges try to involve all the neighboring high schools they can. After all, these local high schools will be sending students to college one day. A favorite device to get high school attention is the collegiate High School Band Day.

In every area and state, some college or university has a traditional High School Band Day each football season, usually in October. The host college invites all the high school bands in the area to be guests on a given Saturday afternoon at one of the big games.

At half-time, all the guest bands come together in the stadium and play a massed-bands show. In some areas, the number of attending bandsmen is so high that the stadium field looks like a sea of band uniforms. It can be a most colorful experience. Musically, its rewards are not great, but as an experience for the high school bandsman it represents a highlight of his band years. At such events every high school bandsman gets to hear and compare hundreds and even thousands of fellow players. It is a social event and gives the bandsman a reward for good work already done in his own marching band.

Neighboring Community Parades and Festivals

There is scarcely a community, town, or city in the country that does not have its own special festivals and parades to accompany them. These are all good chances for a parade band to get out of town and have some fun. It goes without saying that if a band is not a good parade band—that is, if it does not play and march with eye-catching precision and snap—it should not consider going.

But if a band is beautiful in its precision footwork and its ranks march full abreast and its files straight from front to rear, and it has a good, full musical sound on the march, then it should schedule as many out-of-town parade and festival trips as possible.

Plainly put, parades are show-off time. If a band has attractive majorettes, snappy-looking uniforms, a good full instrumentation, a good rhythm section, and plenty of street and parade experience, it should travel as much as finances will allow.

Parade and festival trips do not cost a great deal of money if school buses can be used. However, if the band is so large that it requires the larger commercial charter buses, then costs can become rather high or even prohibitive.

An important point is that if the band becomes good enough, it won't matter how big it is. The financial supporters will find a way somehow to send their band out of town to show it off. Such a band has become an ambassador of goodwill and public relations for the entire community.

This band is playing a rare engagement: it is the first high school band ever to play aboard a U.S. Navy ship.

The Long-Distance Trip

Any overnight trip may be considered long distance. Such an event is a yearly thing with many bands. Overnight trips are expensive, however. They nearly always involve commercial transport and usually the cost of lodgings. But they are major events for the band students who experience them.

Some bands have a long trip on their yearly calendar, but its financing must be planned for a year or more in advance.

XII

~~~~~~

MARCHING BAND

~~~~~~

The Stadium Band: Half-Time Shows

Precision drill is not the most common type of football show. For most bands, it is the hardest show to do well, and it is time-consuming to prepare. The first and absolute requirement is a skilled, experienced director.

Stepping off by twos, fours, etc., is a common drill routine. Training films are available from various music companies to help directors teach this kind of show. They can be rented or purchased and shown to the inexperienced band and the inexperienced director at the same time. They aid greatly in the Casavant drill show. Many directionals and movements are possible by this type of maneuver.

Another kind of marching show is the military drill routine. In military drill, the students must be instructed and drilled more with music. Military commands, maneuvers, directionals, and forms are standard, but they must be taught by oral commands at first. They cannot be dittoed and given to bandsmen as handouts with any success.

Military drill is simply performing various military marching commands to music. It is not easy to teach, and it is difficult for some students to perform. Precision marching is the first goal for such a show. Some standard directionals, steps, and forms are basic. They should be drilled until the band achieves some degree of precision and unity. Then and only then should music be added.

Simple music is best for military drill. With practice, a developing ability at precision marching emerges. As the marching improves, the difficulty of the music may be gradually increased. Some advanced precision marching bands can perform drill to Grade IV marches. This is not easy, and such bands are rare.

As a band becomes skilled in marching precision, it may increase the size, scope, and complexity of its drills. Forms and maneuvers that are eye-catching and fascinating to the stadium audience are endless. Good precision marching bands may spend as much as three hours a school day on the field trying to improve their drill shows. One well-known college marching band has a schedule requiring it to practice on the field five hours every weekday. Needless to say, it is famous and is invited to perform in every major parade of national scope and interest.

The easiest and most effective maneuver for the high school precision marching band is the block drill. This means moving the band in blocks of varying size and shape. The full band may be one block or broken into several inter-blocks.

Block drill moves from the simple to the double and even more complex forms. In every case, music suitable to the particular directional or maneuver is most important. "Just any music" will not do. It must be carefully chosen to match the steps and counts in the drill.

Standard marches are on the decline for this kind of show. Up-to-the-minute popular music is rapidly becoming the thing; the stadium audience appreciates it more. For precision marching purposes, however, 6/8 music lends itself best to step unity. It has a kind of rhythmic swing that 2/4 or 4/4 music does not have.

Regardless of the type of marching band show, a top drill band must practice long and hard to perform successfully in public. The time is well spent, however. The stadium audience gives bouquets every time to a good marching half-time show, and there are other side benefits as well.

The bandsman who can play with strength, volume, and confidence on the march finds stationary playing easy. He has developed his coordination to a high degree. He has better spirit and receives more public recognition and support. He has goodwill from the band audience, and personally he engages in healthful exercise.

Drill band develops legs and rhythmic coordination. Some schools are even moving to accept marching band in lieu of a portion of the required physical education time. Drill band increases awareness of teamwork. It demands acute alertness as to exactly what his fellow bandsmen are doing or playing, or even where they are on the field. The participating drill bandsman has a highly developed sense of audience. This stands him in good stead thereafter, be it in concert, parade, or otherwise. All these factors serve to increase his musicianship and showmanship.

The visual impact of an experienced, well-drilled marching band on the field is tremendous. This impact is intensified if the band uses such simple additional devices as white shoes or white spats, which serve to outline and accentuate the footwork involved.

Pageants

The second major kind of half-time show is the pageant, or production show. Perhaps 80 percent of all high school band half-time shows fall into this category. It includes forming school letters, hearts, flags, showboats, cannons, or other forms.

Letter formations should be mentioned here. They are elementary for high school bands. When a stadium audience has enjoyed a good precision marching band, it should never again accept the school-letter salute to the visiting school half-time show.

Such forms are acceptable only as brief inserted routines into "Bit Drill" or "Perpetual Motion" shows. Majorettes can be very effective in pageant shows; however, they must perform on the field between band and bleachers. Often they steal the thunder of the hard-working band and create ill-feeling thereby.

Standing or stationary forms are effective only in the older, higher concrete bleacher stadiums. These, as far as high school use is concerned, are fast disappearing. In low-bleacher fields, it is impossible to distinguish what forms have been made.

This is one way to get audience attention for a football half-time show.

The "Bit Routine" show is one of the most effective in any stadium. In this show, the band marches in and out, rapidly going from one routine to another, all set to music. This gives variety and change of pace. It also serves to keep an audience watching, listening, and expectantly guessing.

The "Perpetual Motion" show is the crowning achievement for the precision drill band. It requires longer and harder practice than any other kind of show. It is a show that never stops. Music or drum cadence puts the band through its paces without letup. It can be changed in bits. It can be added to. It can be shortened or lengthened at will. It is the most advanced show a stadium band can do. It is also the hardest to work up and perform creditably. The band that succeeds with this type of show will establish a well-deserved and hard-earned reputation.

The Pregame Show

Pregame shows are a must in some areas and districts. In others, they are deemphasized and lackluster. If used, however, each should include the National Anthem. The director immediately has a built-in problem. His show time-slot is tight but floating; that is, he has a certain amount of time to get on and off the field, but the instant he can get on the field is not clearly set or established. It depends on when the warm-up teams clear the field. But the band must be ready to go on signal.

The pregame show must be different from the half-time show. It should use different music and different drills or forms. The wise band director prepares two or at most three pregame routines and alternates these throughout the season. They can be changed a bit from time to time, and with alternation this satisfies the stadium audience.

Bleacher Band

This is a subject of some concern to directors, and chaperones, too, if the game is away from home. The seating of band sections must be traditionalized and allow little movement or interchange of personnel from one section to another. Such interchange can prove embarrassing and even disastrous when the band is called upon to play on such short notice as they usually are in the bleachers.

A few simple rules should be established and followed, with little privilege extended to band members. The band and its sections must sit together for maximum impact when playing in the bleachers. Members must not be allowed to run all over the stadium visiting friends, unless a break period has been given by the director. A lot is expected of bleacher band that many students choose to ignore.

In the first place, bands in the bleachers should be prepared to play something snappy on a second's notice. In order to do this, they must have previously prepared time-out music, or pieces of very short duration (a minute or less). The band should also have set up some comic routines using majorettes and cheerleaders that lend variety and humor to the pigskin pageantry of the occasion. The band should work up some brief brassy fanfare routines to be used with the student body cheering section that will tend to spur the home team on to victory.

Above all, however, for the maximum benefit of everyone in the band, the director, and any accompanying chaperones, the band must retain its sense of discipline and order. Members must remain in place. They must keep their instruments ready to play. And most important of all, bandsmen should play only when called upon by the director. Indiscriminate tootling, blatting, and drumming during bleacher seating at football games should be strictly forbidden. A band that acts up in the bleachers usually has thousands of critics and very few supporters. People like to feel proud of their band. Pride and support go hand in hand.

Parade or Street Band: Power Placement

Street bands should be considered as different from the stadium band. The director must consider his audience. Sections should be placed to create maximum effect and impact upon sideline audience.

Naturally, the street band and the stadium band of a high school will have the same personnel. But the need for powerful impact on the sideline audience calls for different placing of sections within the band.

This rearrangement of placement is usually of great concern, even consternation, to the bandsmen, but it should be no cause for alarm. If bandsmen or sections are changed around, it is to create the best possible impression for the band.

Players in front ranks and last ranks are very important. The outside file players on each side of the band are equally im-

It is not easy to play while taking a bow at a parade reviewing stand.

portant. Their playing is heard and noticed more than the inner-formation members. For this reason, the extreme outside files and the front and back ranks should hold the most experienced and strongest players in the band.

The desired street effect is powerhouse sound and precision footwork. Rhythmic body routines contribute to the visual impact upon the audience. Harmonic thunder, brilliant melody, and a solid, rhythmic beat are qualities of the great street band.

Rhythms in 6/8 time are most fitting to marching. Six-eight rhythms gives the band the best swinging step and movement.

Visual audience impact is further increased by the grooming of the band members. Uniforms should be freshly cleaned and pressed. Hats should be worn at a uniform angle. White web belting and gloves, if used, should be spotlessly white. Polished shoes, white spats, or white shoes themselves make for a neat, trim street band.

Snap, precision arm or instrument movement, or razzle-dazzle add to the great street band on the march. Unfortunately for appearance's sake, some hair, beard, and mustache styles do little to increase a band's appearance.

The sweeping social thrust of the violent 1960's has had no little impact on high school band grooming and physical appearance. Rules and regulations governing hair, grooming, and facial cleanliness have been stretched and ignored in the name of freedom. But this movement has not helped the cause of band in its visual impression on audiences of all types.

XIII

DISCIPLINE VERSUS DISORDER

The Meaning of Discipline

Students hear the word "discipline" many times before entering a performing band. Overall school discipline means one thing. But "band discipline" has a special meaning. That required of a good bandsman in a good band is exceptional, but it is not impossible.

Good discipline is always found in good bands. The accomplishments, invitations to travel and perform publicly, and other musical honors or achievements cannot exist without good discipline in the band.

Therefore, it is important that all potential bandsmen know what it is exactly and specifically. Discipline in band includes conduct, playing, home practice, following director's instructions, and public performance. The good bandsman, in order to contribute the maximum to his fine band, must first discipline himself. The general requirements and demands on a good concert-marching band are many and varied. They, in turn, become requirements of the individual good bandsman.

Talking, idle chatter, or unnecessary noise have no place in a successful band rehearsal. To interfere by any means while music is in progress spoils a rehearsal. It upsets any good director, and once he is angry, the chance for a meaningful rehearsal is slender, indeed. In fact, a rehearsal in which the director is angered by bad conduct can be worse than no rehearsal. It decreases the desired image of the individual band members.

Image

The term "image" is increasingly common in our American vocabulary. Its importance to a band student should be strongly emphasized. Each music student has an image obligation to fulfill. This image of the "good bandsman" is multiplied by the number of members in the band. The overall band image can make or break a band.

This means that each bandsman must be a good egg, a good scout, a good student, and a good, earnest home-practicer. He must be a solid yet inspired citizen in rehearsal. A good performer usually has these easily identifiable qualities.

Attitude

The student's attitude, image, and discipline are all interrelated concerns, and for the high school bandsman they are even more so. He must be receptive to learning music. He is fascinated by his instrument. He is eager to try different kinds of music. He is receptive to whatever direction the band director attempts.

He should be curious about the various elements of music. He tries to become a student leader in band. Student leadership should be a goal of each incoming band student.

It is important that school, community, director, and other bandsmen recognize the well-behaved, studious, and openly receptive instrumental music student. He is invaluable in the high school band world. And he is not as rare as the lesser talent thinks.

In fact, the good bandsman with healthy attitude and good work habits exhibits the right image. He is punctual, loyal, neat, and trim. He is diligent in home practice. He is careful of instruments and equipment.

Furthermore, he is usually openminded when faced with new or different kinds of music. He is active, musical, and works hard at his music. He sacrifices free time for the benefit mutually enjoyed as a member of the fine band he wants to share.

All these qualities compose band discipline. Music in itself demands the most rigorous discipline possible. But there are a number of things discipline is not.

To many, discipline simply means strictness and punishment.

Most bandsmen are proud of their membership in a band with a good image.

Punishment is not discipline. There is a great and important difference between the two. Punishment may result from lapses of discipline. It may follow bad conduct or misbehavior. It may be imposed after deliberate disregard of the requirements, responsibilities, and regulations of band. But punishment is not discipline.

Discipline is the orderly conduct of all band activities. Discipline and punishment may or may not be related in a given band; that is the concern of the director. The student leaders may, in some bands, become involved. This depends on the internal organization of the band itself. In one band, students may be rewarded positively for observing rules and regulations. In another the negative view, or punishment rule, may be in use. A combination of both methods or views may be required. Each situation or organization has its own platform regarding band discipline.

Rewards

The use of rewards appears to be more positive in the area of discipline than does punishment. In regard to a band director, the terms "strong disciplinarian" or "weak disciplinarian" are two common references. A band is said to have "good discipline" or "bad discipline." Such terms are often misleading. Incentives should be studied and compared with the effects of punishment. Band should be made rewarding and purposeful. Its success as a musical organization involves pride and esteem.

The Importance of Discipline

Why is discipline so necessary? Without controlled behavior, effort, and productivity, chaos and disorder would quickly prevail. Anarchy is the order instead of form and order.

A bandsman may fail to see why disciplinary regulations are even necessary. In large bands, the discipline usually is very strict. The increase in size of the band necessitates strong rules and closer observation of them by all members concerned.

Size of band is directly related to discipline. The more people in a closely knit or related group, such as band, the greater the likelihood of more people breaking rules. Once discipline slips, it goes faster and faster. It can disappear entirely.

Discipline is an absolute necessity in a fine musical organization. It is necessary that each band member see the need for it in all areas: in rehearsal, in concert, in transit, and in solitary home practice.

Self-discipline is important. It is the difference between practicing or not practicing at home alone or in school practice rooms. It is the difference between getting something out of such practice and getting nothing from it. Self-discipline is the first required quality of a fine player. He will never reach any musical goal without it.

But then, all roads to goals lead from discipline. Without the disciplined conditioning of each bandsman, no section will perform at the mutually desired high musical level. The band will never reach the goals set by the director. The band will not even reach the desires or ideals of the students themselves.

The individual cannot realize his own potential unless he is disciplined. Self-discipline is the result and the goal combined. A band of well-disciplined individual bandsmen with good attitudes is a joy to behold and to hear. Their respect for and honest desire to improve under the baton of a good director will make their public performances outstanding.

Necessary Participants in Discipline

There are but two active elements involved in band discipline. The first is the student bandsman, the individual. The rewards of good discipline are great and lasting. To participate in band in an atmosphere of anything less than good discipline is illogical and unrewarding, to say the least.

The band student's gains are great if all concerned work to full capacity, effort, and ability. An atmosphere of poor, weak, or bad discipline is indefensible by student, director, school, or parents.

The second necessary element in the world of discipline is the band director. He sets the tone in and out of the band room for band in his community. He determines what he will or will not allow. He decides what will go into creating the kind of band he intends to have.

If the school administration does not support the band director in his efforts or his discipline, however, the band is lost. Many school administrations have set up recent networks of school policy that do not prove to be positive support for the school band programs. Where school policy concerned with political peace allows privileges or discretionary loopholes for certain students with extenuating circumstances, the band is frequently in a state of turmoil. In these circumstances, the band director is powerless; his discipline and control are weakened immeasurably.

The Strict Disciplinarian

Some band students may mistakenly assume that the band director is a harsh disciplinarian because he enjoys it. This is rarely true. The "strict disciplinarian" usually results when unruly individuals or groups make it necessary.

The typically fine band director is interested in producing and expressing beautiful music, getting it from his students, if possible. His chief aim is a fine band of top instrumentalists who can create the mood a musical composition inspires. To involve himself with harsh disciplinary measures destroys a director's efforts. It negates much of his instruction, it destroys his rapport with his students, and it undermines his hope for success in his musical and social efforts.

Yet, most fine directors recognize the necessity of good discipline in their bands. A strong band is founded on fair and effective discipline, but it does not have to be harsh. This must be understood until the conditions of discipline become second nature in the band. Discipline must become a tradition before a band can be considered a good one. These two ideas are inseparable and indivisible.

A band of mediocre or lax discipline will be mediocre or worse as a performing unit. Bands with good discipline fulfill their goals.

A vast host of people support discipline in a band. The school principal usually supports the director. Faculty rules and regulations that govern the school apply equally to the band. Band parents are even more important. Band mothers and fathers invariably support good discipline and the director in order to have a good band.

XIV

~~~~~~

BAND RESPONSIBILITIES

~~~~~~

Responsibilities to Self

Each new or experienced bandsman has a responsibility to his own talent. Once this capability has been tested, outlined, and proved, the bandsman must begin to work with it. He owes it to himself to develop this talent. It must be explored to find who he is musically. Who he is capable of becoming musically is a lifelong challenge.

The development and exploration of one's talent should be fun and not work. It should, however, be approached with workmanlike determination. Talent does not develop in a vacuum. Practice is one of the first major responsibilities of the talented bandsman.

Practice is done in private. Regardless of place, be it basement, school practice room, or his room at home, he must practice. His potential must be developed to its fullest. But it is essential that a bandsman with talent know how to practice correctly. Concentration is the secret and the key. One must concentrate on specifics.

The daily practice fare is scales, broken chords, phrasing, breath control, tonguing, dynamics, and good tone. But one must also concentrate on specific problems. Difficult passages in music under study are an important area of daily practice. There are all sorts of musical difficulties to be worked through, controlled, or mastered.

Musical problem-solving is the purpose of practice. But to succeed, the student must clearly understand what he is trying to accomplish. He must face his musical problems and identify them. How to practice can often be a real problem in itself. In that case, the band director can help the student relate successfully to his practice assignments.

Responsibility to Music

The band student has a definite responsibility to music in his later life. High school bandsmen are chiefly concerned with their band. They relate to the music at hand. They deal with the band activities, the director, and their school. Yet during the "good old days" in band, most think now and then of life after high school.

Many expect to be merely musical consumers. Some want to become professionals in other fields and to have music as an avocation.

Some few music students choose music as a livelihood. Such bandsmen have a responsibility to get the most from their high school band training and experience. The responsibility in this area is to determine where one wants to go. The next step is to prepare for it.

Responsibility to Other Bandsmen

Each student owes a debt to all the other players in his section. His own contribution matters, but it would be meaningless without the combined effort of his fellow section members. Each section player should, therefore, play his own part to its fullest. He has a responsibility to compete within the section. The section playing level must be raised; at no time should it be considered as tops.

A student may feel his own part is small, and his contribution may seem unimportant. But a full, great band sound is composed of all players playing their parts, interweaving them together. Music is thus a tapestry of sound, of tone.

Responsibility to Student Conductors

If the band has student-assisted conductors, it is advanced and fortunate. Such student conductors often lack the skills they need or would like to have. The player under the baton of the student director has a definite responsibility. He should be

A good drum major is the field director of a football band while in the bleachers.

doubly alert to anticipate the baton movements. Supporting the student director can only win friends and influence others to follow suit.

It is a definite musical challenge to student musicians to play under student conductors. Such an assistant represents the band director. If a doubtful moment arrives the playing musician has only one question to ask of himself: what would he do if the director had the baton?

Most well-organized bands have student officers. They may

be duly elected presidents, vice-presidents, secretaries, treasurers, librarians, or others. The playing bandsman is responsible for relating to each fairly and honestly.

In some bands, the officers are appointed by the director. They may be and should be selected because of ability. Popularity should not be entirely overlooked, however. The student officer has a responsibility to the bandsmen with whom he works. In each case and band, the student soon learns that there are followers and leaders.

The new bandsman should adapt and become agreeable with his student leaders. They may be section leaders, student conductors, squad leaders, drum majors, or precision drillmasters. He learns to follow the director. Only when a student has learned to follow the band leaders is he capable of a leadership position himself.

Responsibility to the Director

The band member's prime responsibility is to the band director. This is the first concern of the good instrumentalist. It is up to the student to absorb, observe, and learn the conductor's baton technique. There are but a few basics of baton movements, but there are as many variations as there are band directors.

The band student's goal should be to elevate the band into a higher playing level. That is the same goal the director has. Cooperation is the key word. A director-versus-student situation achieves little that is worthy of note or distinction.

Responsibility to Practical and Physical Property

The high school bandsman is directly responsible in certain physical and practical areas of band life. The care and maintenance of his instrument are all-important matters. The uniform, its appearance, shoes, spats, hat, and gloves are of no little concern to the proud bandsman.

His equipment and music are all expensive items; he is responsible for their usage and care. The rehearsal chair area where he sits is his to police and keep clean and neat. A fresh, neat band rehearsal room immediately puts the band in a sense of cleanliness. If all is in place, individual students tend to treat surroundings and property with more respect, and equipment and materials last longer. Rehearsals tend to go off better in clean, neat rehearsal rooms.

Responsibility to the School

The student body is a community in itself. The bandsman owes his classmates his best as a member of their band. The longer the band has been established and the more traditional it is, the greater is the responsibility of the individual members to its good name and repute.

The student body is composed of organizations, teams, and clubs. The band student must consider these groups. They can be meaningful to him and the band, either helping or hindering. Pleasant working relations with school clubs and teams increase the fun of band work. Conflicts tend to degrade band in the eyes of the school.

The principal and assistants are important cogs in the school machinery. The bandsman must keep good relations with them. The administration can make or break a band program. If a friendly atmosphere exists between band and administrators, the band usually receives many good things other bands may not.

The director's fellow faculty members usually have an eye on the band and him. Even if they are not all music lovers, they will support the band if a friendly relationship exists. It is the responsibility of each bandsman to work toward producing such a solid situation.

The faculty of a school can destroy a band by simply failing to cooperate. A good band receives many requests to leave the school on playing or concert trips. Without a friendly faculty arranging makeup assignments for the traveling band members, the band will suffer. Top academic students will not even want to travel with the band if an unfriendly faculty is going to penalize them with extra assignments on their return.

Responsibility to Band Boosters

Such clubs are usually made up of band parents. Other community well-wishers and music lovers will belong, too. These people are directly involved with trying to support their band. They are behind most if not all projects and activities. The bandsmen have a responsibility to earn their support in financing trips, festivals, and other fun travel.

These followers of bands and band music increase the bandsman's morale. That, in itself, is a very important matter in band work. Their financial support may send the band on its merry way when trip time comes. Their backing in many other ways helps the band to progress and even to survive in hardship situations. Bands without booster clubs usually are undeveloped and relatively inactive.

Responsibility to the Community

Every community, whatever its size, is a group of groups. The bandsman should know these groups, the organizations or civic bodies within his community. He should make himself responsible to them. These clubs and civic bodies will thereafter support a good band. But their support and backing will equal the esteem and goodwill built up by the individual bandsmen and the director.

A bandsman would do well to be slightly political. He should consider that everyone in his community belongs to some group. No citizen is alone. An investment of responsible interest on the bandsman's part will yield returns far beyond his expectations. Community support is the difference between a lackluster, mediocre band program and a good or even great one.

This band enjoyed a band booster club of seven hundred members, who financed their travels.

Problems and Solutions

An advancing bandsman learns to accept certain basic truths in band work. There are problems. But the key to problem-solving is viewpoint. How does the bandsman view the problem? No problem is insoluble. A change of view usually helps.

In reality, there are no problems; there are only opportunities. What seems to be a problem is, in reality, the opportunity for that bandsman to see how he can overcome it. Thus, it becomes a challenge, and everyone should accept a challenge. If a bandsman can learn to view his problems as opportunities to show his wits and intelligence, he will have no problems. He will have only opportunities, solutions, and a host of amazed friends, well-wishers, and supporters.

XV

MUSICAL ECOLOGY

Our World of Sound: Music and Tone

Ecology is a common word in today's vocabulary. Our natural environment is a national issue. It even has political overtones.

But so far, the term has neglected the bandsman's favorite and immediate world: his music. The world of sound is the instrumentalist's arena.

He may live on the edge of a wildlife preserve. His community may be devoted to protecting the natural environment. But how does it happen that Americans have so long ignored an environment in which everyone exists.

Everyone with hearing ability shares the aural or sound world. Most of us hear too much, and most of what we hear is too loud. Most dangerous of all, most of what we hear we could live far better without. Sound can be measured in decibels, units of volume or degrees of loudness. Above a certain decibel level, sound becomes unpleasant. At a higher decibel plateau, sound becomes intolerable.

Loud sounds pound our ears from every direction. Listening regularly to extremely loud sounds over a long period of time will deafen the listener.

Usually young listeners of extremely loud electric rock instruments discredit this warning. But rock music lovers who have their electric instruments turned up to an unreasonably high decibel level are steadily going deaf.

The process is so gradual that such students or players do not realize their worsening condition. But rock music is in the forefront of the "deafening" world of sound. Rock music lovers and musicians alike argue that their music must be loud to be good, that it is "supposed" to be played above a certain volume.

That is a common defense, but no thinking musician will agree with it. Extremely high volume filling a room even vibrates the walls and floors. It pounds on the human eardrums.

COURTESY *THE CREATIVE WORLD* OF STAN KENTON

The famous Stan Kenton has bridged any generation gap with this jazz appearance at Interlocken Music Camp in Michigan.

It certainly does affect the listener, but the effects are not all that good. Deafness is the end result. The time comes when the player, listener, or consumer of such loud music demands that it be louder and louder; only then will he really be able to hear it and feel it. When that time comes, the ear involved ignores all of lesser volume. Partial deafness is a milestone to total deafness.

This is not to say that all rock music is bad. Many rock passages, themes, lyrics, and melodies are beautiful. Harmonies and rhythms in the rock idiom are often pleasant. Many selections conform to the forms of standard and traditional music. But the usual volume level demanded by rock musician and rock listener is another story.

To decrease the volume of such music brings down the wrath or ridicule of rock lovers in general. The so-called "generation gap" rears its ugly head. Another name for "generation gap" might well be "decibel gap," or "aural gap," or, worse yet, "deafness gap."

Popular music in general uses passages of contrasting volume, which lend variety to musical expression. But on the rock scene, the volume is usually at maximum and unchanging. Above a certain decibel level, however, music vanishes, and sound merely becomes unbearable noise.

Aural Pollution

We live in a world of sound. It is universal for those who can still hear. For those who are deaf or who are, by choice, growing deaf, the world of sound is being shut out.

The human ear is a unique mechanism. Under continued bombardment of extremely loud sound, the ear adjusts: it shuts itself off. Eventually it accepts nothing below a certain level of volume. It has become deaf to a certain amount of the sound world. With continued subjection to great volume, it eventually shuts out everything. At that time, the person involved is totally deaf. His ear has protected itself to the point where it accepts nothing.

America's National Unconsciousness

Young rock music lovers are not alone, however, in their obsession with objectionable volume. Most Americans exist in a state of national unconsciousness to sound. Our country is obsessed with sound.

We must have sound in every office, building, restaurant, or wherever people congregate. Why? Who can define silence? Worse yet, who can even find it?

Americans have to go far afield to escape the national pastime of piped-in sound. Early piped-in sound was more melodious than it is now. As time passes, such "music" does not necessarily get better, but it is getting louder.

Americans cannot enjoy a meal, a picnic, or a beach party, or even have a tooth pulled without piped-in music. Whatever happened to silence? It is safe to say that many of the young generation of bandsmen do not know what silence really means. They have never enjoyed it. We have all lived with continual sound so long that silence itself has become unknown.

In the concert world, composers and musicians know the value of silence. Frequent measures of total silence or rest occur in music. They strengthen or underscore what follows. Silence, thus, is a balance to sound. Continued sound without the relief of silence becomes monotonously hypnotic.

Musical sound balanced by measures of absolute silence becomes meaningful. Variety and change in music are important. The hearer or listener will try to listen more carefully. Sound and silence should both be on every set of musical scales. That applies equally to city symphony, high school band, or popular restaurant.

The Changing Band Literature

Many young bandsmen reject music dated before their own time. Music for them must be *now* music, up to the minute, and no older than this year's styles.

Why should this be true? The answer may be found in the tonal effects used in musical eras. They change, going forward and backward. They really go in cycles or circles. Tonal effects are used, discarded, forgotten, and then rediscovered. Now and then someone even discovers a new tonal combination.

But why must the old be discarded from the band literature? Why narrow and limit the literature to the days of the bandsman concerned? Many students actually express dislike for music published before "now." Such players would dump everything and buy fresh, new music each school year.

Finance alone would make this impossible. Band directors must keep a library of music they have purchased over the years. All the music played on a given concert cannot be purchased new for that year's program. Yet many band students expect such conditions to prevail. But such student demands are based on the tonal effects used in the newer and changing band literature.

This view and situation have created a problem for band music composers. They are forced to create modern effects that the young bandsman will accept. Older tonal colors in band music used traditional and long-established instrumentation. Tonal color depends at all times on instrumental combinations.

The band instrumentation has changed little over the years of its existence. It has used the same instruments in the main: trumpets, trombones, baritone horns, tubas, French horns, bass clarinets, alto clarinets, contra-alto and contrabass clarinets, flutes, piccolos, oboes, bassoons, snare drums, bass drums, tympani, marimbas, bells, gongs, and various other novelty equipment.

These instruments make up what has become accepted as the standard band instrumentation. From time to time, new equipment appears. The synthesizer, octave or harmonic amplifier, and the electric guitar are relatively new. So far, however, their use in concert or symphonic band has ranged from little to none. An altonium, bell-front style was introduced in the recent past. One band instrument manufacturer produced an alto trombone. It would be almost impossible to find either of these instruments in practical use in high school bands today, and yet they would be useful and welcome additions.

How does the band composer of today solve the problem of student interest? It has not been easy. The only road open to composer and arranger alike has been to use new or unusual combinations of instruments.

Older and more traditional arrangements used sectional effects. One section or another in variation or together produced aural or tonal effects. Today the composer or arranger may split up the standard sections. He may double instruments in some new or vivid combination to capture student player and listener interest.

How Band Will Change the Bandsman

Technical advancement does not come all at once. It comes slowly. Often the student hardly realizes it. But technical achievement and skills develop with practice. Musical awareness increases. Membership in band changes the student's outlook.

In a good band, the change will be for the better. A bandsman becomes more acutely aware of the music he plays. He knows what is going on in the music he hears. By hearing and playing musical effects, the band student expands his world of sound.

This development, called critical faculty, helps him know the difference between the good and the bad. The bandsman develops a high degree of critical faculty. His musical band experience takes him through many musical journeys.

He learns to recognize effects, rhythm patterns, and melodies. Thus, his appreciation for all music increases. This appreciation growth is a natural development of an active high school bandsman. As his background of musical experience increases, he learns to appreciate what he hears in the music of others. Such a student tends to outgrow the "rock world" that is so often the entire aural world of high school. This increasing appreciation accepts concert music, pop music, country music, even symphonic music, and an ever enlarging circle of instrumental music.

Piccolo and flute players develop acute faculties to hear themselves playing in the parade thunder.

This puts such a student beyond the narrow confines of rock music. He learns by experience that the world of music is all related. There is basically little difference between sacred and secular, between popular and concert. Music is music. It all contains the same basic elements: harmony, melody, rhythm, volume variation or dynamics, expression, and consonance or dissonance.

A student's current life and his future life in countless ways are enriched by his band experience. The bandsman who plays in and graduates from a fine, active high school band is a rich man. His riches are in the aural world. It is one in which we all must live, but it becomes his first world.

In later years this does not change or even lessen. If anything, it increases with time and age. That is his legacy and his heritage from high school band. Where else can one get as much?

XVI

FUND-RAISING FOR FUN

Fun Expenses

Festival trips and other travels of the band cost money. Although every school pays part of the band's upkeep, no school pays all of it.

Regional and state band festival trips are usually paid out of the school budget. In some cases, however, the school may not have enough money to budget its band.

But not all festivals are school- or state-related. Some are fun festivals. Every state in the union has any number of these. The experienced marching band will usually try to enter one of these every year, if financially possible.

A quick look at a list of festivals will show their purpose or nature. Some are of national stature or prominence; for instance, the Pasadena Parade of the Roses, Macy's Christmas Parade in New York, the Philadelphia Mummers, the Chicagoland Music Festival, the Orange Bowl Parade in Miami, and the Memphis Cotton Carnival.

There are many interesting regional festivals bands may enter in their own areas if they have the finances to do so. In the mid-eastern states, for example, one could go to the Norfolk Azalea Festival, the Washington Cherry Blossom Festival, the Virginia Beach Band Festival, Myrtle Beach, the Tampa Gasparilla, the Winchester (Virginia) Apple Blossom Festival, or the West Virginia Mountain State Forest Festival.

Whatever the region, the bandsman may rest assured that nearby there is an interesting and lively festival parade that needs and wants good marching bands. A letter to the state chamber of commerce will provide the necessary information.

Unless the festival is local, however, the school will not sponsor the band's transportation, housing, or other expenses. Any one of these items can be large or small, depending upon how far away the festival is and how large the band is.

Transportation

Travel cost is usually the big problem with distant festival trips. The usual mode is bus. School buses may take the band to nearby affairs, but travel of any distance, and particularly across state lines, usually demands chartered buses. The larger the band, the more buses required. It should be noted that the bus is the least expensive means of transporting a band.

But who pays the fare? Schools will not. It becomes necessary for the band to raise the money. Trips of more than six or seven hundred miles should involve either rail or air: these cost more than buses, but they are faster and allow the band more fun time once at its destination.

Raising money for train or air travel becomes a major problem. More people must become involved. The band members alone cannot raise this kind of money.

On all overnight fun festival travel, housing is the next cost to consider. Where will the band spend the night? Is there sufficient housing at the festival area? What will it cost? How will the band finance that?

The Band Booster Club

The band without an active boosters club has two strikes against it when it starts to raise money. Some school administrators favor band booster clubs, but others do not. In the latter case, the band has severe fund-raising problems, but they should never be considered impossible.

The band booster club is essential in large fund-raising efforts. It also serves as a chaperone pool for overnight stays. Adult chaperones are necessary on the road, in hotels, motels, or fun centers. They play a very important part in fun festival trips. They see to the general welfare and well-being of the individual band members assigned to them in team groups.

But who pays their way? Chaperone housing and transportation costs are paid from funds raised by the band for the entire event. Most experienced band chaperones expect these costs to be covered. They usually are more than willing to pay their personal expenses, such as food and incidentals.

Recreational Trips

Many band booster clubs believe strongly in rewarding their bands for their hard work during the school year. Often a club will take the band to a professional baseball or football game, usually some distance away.

Most school administrators willingly approve a one-day trip to such events. Many or most, however, balk if such fun travel involves overnight stay. Unless such a trip had some measure of educational value or experience, it would likely be unapproved by the administration.

The wise band director should arrange educational tours near the athletic event, which help to justify the cost involved. Historical spots, museums, homes of Presidents, or certain modern scenes can become important sites, adding weight to the trip purpose and serving to ward off criticism of band travel or its costs.

The ideal solution is for the band to be invited to perform at half-time. Principals who would not approve such trips for their school band are rare. In fact, they usually are more than eager to go along to such events. In any case, it will be necessary for the band to raise money for the trip.

As for fun festivals, in some cases the band will play in a colorful parade. Bands, clowns, funny men, floats, and pretty girls are the order of the day. But again, a wise director will add weight to his trip. He can do this by scheduling a well-publicized lawn concert at the event, or he might put on a night program of regular concert proportions. Such programs serve as added incentives for the band to work up new music. Students practice more and thus are motivated to become better musicians and bandsmen.

Concert Instruments

Some bands must raise money to pay for certain symphonic instruments: oboes, bassoons, double French horns, good baritones, upright tubas, alto or bass clarinets, contra alto or bass clarinets, baritone saxophones, altoniums, tympani, and even piccolos.

If the band hopes for musical greatness, it must have all the instruments called for in the musical score. The cost of such instruments rises yearly. If the school cannot afford them, who will pay for them?

Before a parents' or nonparents' booster club will work for such things, their importance must be heavily emphasized by the band director. He must make known their need and importance to the band.

He may not get such instruments all at once, but planned purchasing should be arranged. Yearly purchases can be made. With money raised by regular means or anticipated sources, the instruments can be purchased on a year-to-year schedule.

Instrumental Replacement and Repair

The school pays for ordinary wear and tear on instruments and equipment. Once again, however, the budget limits the spending on such items. The usual budget does not cover all replacement or repair costs. If not, the band may add such costs to its own fund-raising activities. Such things, however, detract from funds raised for fun trips and festivals.

Other Band Operational Costs

Printed concert programs and tickets cost money. Some school print shops can do this work free. Others have problems preventing such work from being done for all school organizations. Then it becomes necessary to go to a local print shop.

Good printing is not cheap, but such costs can easily be handled by a knowledgeable band director. Where school policy permits, he should be able to get local merchant advertising to pay the costs. Advertisements on school concert programs or tickets are good business.

The wise director will have cultivated such donors or advertisers who can be called upon to help on a moment's notice.

Awards and Publicity

Publicity photos, band handbooks, awards, trophies, plaques or prizes can all be paid for or supplied by local businessmen. If advertisements are impossible, public recognition will often spur such donations.

However, the cost of honors, organizational insignia, or scholarships will not often be paid by businessmen or the school.

National awards such as the Arion Award and the John Philip Sousa Award, Best Musician, or the Director's Award can become yearly and regular costs. Band stripes, service bars, and even summer or regular scholarships are common financial goals of good bands with booster clubs. Without a band booster group to help, the band is at a loss for most of its extras.

Cost of summer music or band camp is often paid by the

booster club. These experiences are a typical financial goal of an active booster club. They are fun jaunts for the lucky bandsman who gets the financial support of a booster club; they are also educational and musically rewarding.

Ways of Earning Money

Concerts are the most common way a band has to earn money. A good band with aggressive leadership and organization can raise a surprising amount of money at a band concert, but it is not easy. Tickets must be pushed at every corner and opportunity.

An increased audience at concerts can be guaranteed by offering door prizes or numbered ticket drawings. The door prizes can be donated by local business. The better the prize, the better the ticket sale and the more money the band realizes for its fun and travel.

Football Stadium Income

Several fund-raising means relate to the football stadium. A good, busy band can raise money during football season. In fact, it must, if later events are to take place. Some of these activities are fun and rewarding. However, to share in money from any or all of these sources requires the utmost diplomacy from the director and the booster club.

Some long-established bands have worked their way up to a share in the stadium gate receipts. Some bands get from 5 to 10 percent of the net gate receipts; these bands should press for their percentage to be from the gross.

Bands not receiving a share of the gate receipts should work toward that goal. Good pregame and half-time shows with a large, appreciative stadium audience help to achieve this financial support.

Festivals are girls, bands, and music.

Concession stands and the sale of game programs, popcorn, hot chocolate, coffee, stadium cushions, and flags are all money-makers for the active band. School policy must be worked out by the director. Band boosters, administrators, and football personnel must agree on the band's importance and share the gate receipts.

Sales Campaigns

A number of commercial companies are active in the fund-raising field for school bands. The company organizer comes in and handles all details. The time of the campaign is compressed to a very short sale and collection time. Prizes are the order for the best sales teams. These professional fund-raising concerns account for a remarkable amount of money raised for band finance.

Handling Fund-Raising Receipts

Immediate collection of all money is of the utmost importance; daily collections should be effected. Loss and theft take a big bite of sales and collections in every campaign. Strict accounting methods must be set up. Students must be accountable for their collected money.

XVII

AN ILLUSTRIOUS PAST

Early American Bands

One of the first bands in America played in New York City in the 1630's. Unlike today's large instrumentation, that band had four instruments: a trumpet, a flute, a violin, and a drum.

Small German bands and gutter bands developed in New England until 1773. Josiah Flagg gave concerts in Faneuil Hall, Boston, with America's first band of any size; it had fifty men.

As bands grew in American towns, they outdid themselves with brilliant uniforms, plumes, epaulets, and big hats with flowers or ribbons. Almost every town had a band. Many of the musicians could not read music, but they loved it. Many were quite accomplished on their instruments. They gave pleasure and delight to a growing musical public.

Military bands delighted George Washington and Benjamin Franklin alike. The famous "Spirit of Seventy-Six" picture of the revolutionary fife and drum was real in colonial times. These bands were called "Droom and Foof" bands.

The Official U.S. Marine Band

In 1794 Congress began to organize service bands in earnest. President John Adams signed a bill to form the Official Marine Band in 1798. The band was made up of a drum major, a fife major, and thirty-two drums and fifes.

Today's Official U.S. Marine Band first played in Philadelphia and then moved to Washington. President Thomas Jefferson was called the "godfather" of the band after it marched in review on the first Fourth of July celebration in Washington in 1801.

RAY DICKENSON PHOTO

A good, big high school band today may march 135 members.

Concert Bands

The golden age of American band music was opened by a Frenchman, Louis Antoine Jullien. His Boston and New York concerts in 1853–54 set style and tone for all who followed him.

Jullien, born in 1812, the son of a military bandmaster, had studied at the famous Paris Conservatory. He was a talented and accomplished musician. He also loved and put on musical extravaganzas such as the world had never seen before.

Jullien's band played from a library of thousands of brilliant pieces. The players were the world's best, and Jullien was the showman to end all showmen. He used large bands of more than a hundred players and attention-getting devices nobody had thought of at concerts. Fire engines raced with bells clanging; fireworks went off; two bands played in different keys; miniature locomotives on the stage streamed black-wool smoke. Jullien used the "world's largest bass drum."

Jullien was colorful and dramatic; he appealed to the old and the young. Pat Gilmore was such a young musician. He aspired to equal or exceed Jullien.

Pat Gilmore was twenty-three years old when Jullien retired to his European home with his vast profits. Pat organized his first band and soon outdid his idol. During the next thirty years he was the most famous bandmaster in America, becoming known as "the Father of the American Band."

From Gilmore to Sousa

Fittingly enough, in America, a land of international minorities, Pat Gilmore was born in Ireland. He first played in regimental bands in the British Isles. Drifting to Canada, he later went to Boston, where he led the famed Boston Brigade Band.

He served in the Civil War with his band. In 1864 in Louisiana, he staged a dramatic effort marking his own style. He put together a school chorus of 5,000, a 500-piece band, a huge drum and fife corps, and used bells and cannons in patriotic music such as "Hail Columbia" and "America."

In his heyday, his concerts included anvils clanging, sparks flying, cannons firing by electricity, and 100-piece bands. After the great Chicago fire, Pat Gilmore's band celebrated the restoration of "The Windy City." His band played concerts in the huge concourse of the Lake Shore Railroad station, a room two blocks long that held 40,000 people. At that time his band had about 300 members and a chorus of 1,000 singers.

Sousa

Two days after Gilmore died at the St. Louis Exposition on September 24, 1892, John Philip Sousa directed the first concert of his very own band. Thus began forty years of America's greatest bandmaster's career. Sousa was then twenty-six years old.

When he began to direct the U.S. Marine Band in 1880 he was so young that he grew a heavy black beard to make himself look older to his older musicians who had once played for his father. Sousa had begun as a violinist, but he drifted into military bands because during the Civil War he was strongly attracted to them.

He developed the Marine Band into a fine musical organization and led the way for symphonic music for military bands. Sousa toured the world with his own New Marine Band later. He earned a fortune and was by far the most famous bandmaster in the world.

Sousa's band was launched at the Chicago World's Fair. There he pioneered in the audience "sing-along" with vast crowds, using "The Old Folks at Home." He also introduced and popularized his own brilliant band arrangements of "After the Ball" and "Ta-Ra-Ra-Boom-Der-E."

Sousa was a brilliant musician, a gifted composer, and a superior showman. He surrounded himself with America's and Europe's finest musicians. He filled America's ears with music they could recognize, love, and applaud. He was, in all probability, one of America's greatest educators, but he was not so by choice or goal. He was fond of telling educator friends, "You are an educator. I am an entertainer."

A New Kind of Music

During the peak of the great concert bands of Sousa and others, a music filtered out of bordellos that was to alter the entire music world forever. Jazz and ragtime came out into the streets. Jazz bands played in New Orleans funeral processions. Jazz sounded in saloons and on Mississippi riverboats. Little bands formed and played the new music. It was fresh and enthusiastic.

Audiences for the great concert bands began to feel its thrust. Sousa included jazz on his programs. The American public began to go "jazz, ragtime, blues, and dixieland" in its popular taste.

This music was spread by a new device. Thomas A. Edison's phonograph that had recorded the brilliant Sousa and others began also to record the new jazz. The effect of these bands and their music spread rapidly. The paying public began to drift to jazz, rather than to continue supporting their military bands and their music.

Municipal Bands

By 1912 nearly every American town of any size had its own band. Some towns and cities levied a special tax to support the band. It became an American tradition. Free concerts thrilled the local public. Bands flourished around the country. An American Bandmasters' Association was formed. Parades sprouted like wild flowers. Military music had the beat for marching bands. It was made for it.

Allentown, Pennsylvania; Barrington, New Hampshire; Long Beach, California; and Fort Dodge, Iowa were cities with important bands.

Industrial Bands

One of the oldest bands sponsored by industry was the Altoona, Pennsylvania, band of the Pennsylvania Railroad. The Missouri-Kansas and Texas sponsored bands. Bands of Ford

Motors, the Willys-Overland Auto Company, John Wanamaker in New York City, Caterpillar Tractor, and the American Rolling Mill Company of Middletown, Ohio, played fairs, parades, and hometown programs.

Today's band music includes military marches, pop, jazz, rock, concert, and symphonic.

Salvation Army Bands

In 1878 the Fry family joined William Booth's English Salvation Army and came to America. They made up a brass quartette. This soon led to "banding" in the Salvation Army, a program that grew into a strong, well-organized structure.

Headed by a band sergeant, the band-members have rigorous expectations, rehearsals, and engagements. There are three grades of Salvation Army bands. The students graduate as officers. One famous American trumpeter and bandleader, Harry James, once played in a Salvation Army band.

Circus Bands

Merle Evans, the leader of the Ringling Brothers–Barnum and Bailey Circus band, is the most famous circus band leader ever known. He has been called the "Toscanini of the Big Top." He is highly respected and is a guest conductor much in demand, even at such symphonically inclined places as the famous Interlocken Music Camp in Michigan.

College Bands

Dr. Albert A. Harding, Illinois University band director for forty-three years, is an outstanding early college figure. He was so admired by Sousa that at Sousa's death in 1932 his great library of band compositions went to the Illinois University band.

By then the college band program was long under way, and it had great need for students. Feeder schools became important. Where would great college bands get good music students?

The American High School Band

Early high school bands really began to multiply about the time of World War I. As jazz blossomed in the 1920's and Sousa and the professional concert bands faded out in the 1930's, high school bands grew and flourished.

Many early high school bandmasters were from the military bands of the past. They had been so trained, and they continued their tradition in their high school bands. A national band contest in 1923 sponsored by music manufacturers and giving money prizes set off the development of band contests. From this date, United States bands changed. The school instrumental music program was off with a bang.

A School Band Pioneer

Archie McAllister, born on a farm near Joliet, Illinois, sold a pet pig to buy a cornet. He later organized his own schoolboy band, worked for a street-car company, and went west. But at last he returned to teach manual training in Chicago and then in Joliet High School.

Archie McAllister's cornet looked something like this.

He loved band music, but he had no formal music training. Nevertheless, in the first national school band contest in Chicago, McAllister's Joliet High School Band won first place. In fact, it won first place so often that finally it was barred from entering so that others would have a chance to win.

This famous first band directed by an untrained leader won many state and national contests. It finally received the first national school band trophy ever awarded on the international scene. The band played a week's engagement at the Radio City Music Hall, at the Metropolitan Opera House, in Washington, and in Philadelphia.

When McAllister died in 1944 he was honored by thousands. A modest man, he had created one of the greatest high school bands in the world. The record of this great organization still stands today. Few achieve its level.

XVIII

CAREERS AND OPPORTUNITIES
IN BAND

Advice for Graduating Senior Bandsmen

The graduating senior bandsman is concerned about his future. What is in store for him? Will he rise, or fail? Succeed? And at what? Will his band work be a part? Can it help?

The answer in a nutshell is, it can do a great deal. If the bandsman wants a career in music, his high school band can do a very great deal. It may be the springboard into his musical future. How much can it help him? That depends on the student.

Self-Evaluation

The student can get a clear picture of things by taking a good look at himself. Has he contributed to his band greatly, or little? Has he been a leader or a follower? Has he worked or shirked in band? Has he reached any real degree of technical ability or musical style on his instrument?

Has he enjoyed every minute of band—even the extra drill, the rehearsals, and the repetition and endless practice, the blood, sweat, and tears of festival competition? Has he developed musically, technically, and in appreciation after all his years in band?

Does he love his instrument? Band music? Band work? Has he observed his band director closely enough to see fairly clearly into the field?

The great, important summary question is: after all the band student has been through in his band, how does he regard such "pursuit of excellence"?

If the bandsman has been a strong player on his instrument, has successfully competed in regional and state competitions, and has been a diligent, loyal, long-practicing musical leader and officer in an active, concert-traveling band, then he might well consider a career in some area of band work.

The first questions facing the strongly interested bandsman at this point are what bands are there after high school, and how could he make a living in the field?

Bands in the Pop Music World

Bands are like bees in a hive: they are all over the place, particularly rock bands. Cock an ear toward any suburban basement. A rock band is practicing there. It may be small, but it most certainly will be loud.

The chances are it sounds horrible—at first. But even in this case, practice makes perfect, or, at least, it may make it perfectly acceptable one day. It will certainly lead to improvement.

One should always remember: from little rock bands great rock bands grow. The zero money they earn in the beginning can lead to personal incomes in the hundreds of thousands of dollars.

The unknown rock musician thundering away in his basement may one day "hit the big time." Some rock stars own private jet planes, their own record companies, music publishing companies, their own clubs, or a chain of franchised operations.

Many rock band leaders and musicians go on into motion pictures or television. When rock bands play, they are playing some composer's composition, or some arranger's arrangement. A fine career can be based on composing alone. Its financial rewards can be very great today.

A handful of hits, and the composer may become financially

independent. Arrangers are not always the highest earners, but the experienced arranger soon turns out his own compositions. In such a case, his income from record royalties suddenly leaps upward.

The large dance bands and popular orchestras are an area of the pop music career to consider. Although there are not as many as formerly, the existing ones must employ good instrumentalists. The fast-rising high school stage band program will feed musicians into this field.

Band leaders such as Stan Kenton and other famous "names" lead today in jazz education on many college campuses. A large amount of their musical activity is involved with collegiate jazz festivals and clinics. Some of these famous bands are large. Combined royalties from recording, arrangements, compositions, public performances, and other sources help pay the salaries of their musicians.

Leaders, sidemen, and the instrumentalists playing under the leader's baton are all trained musicians. Where did they get their training? Most, if not all, at one time played in a high school band.

Military Bands

The U.S. Marine Band is the oldest and most renowned service band in America. Musicians in this band enjoy instrumental careers that are extraordinary. It is a world unto itself, a colorful life full of music, travel, excitement, and financial stability. It is *the* top band in America. It has been famous since Sousa's time.

The U.S. Navy Band ranks just as high in musicianship, musical taste, and importance. While its tradition is not that of the Marine Band, it is also a top band. Its members are all superb instrumentalists. They, too, lead a good life as full-time musicians and Navy personnel. The U.S. Navy School of Music is *the* important link in the service military band program.

The U.S. Army Band is equal to the Navy and Marine bands. Only the finest players make it into the ranks of this band; the reputation, career, and livelihood are to be envied.

The U.S. Air Force Band is the newest of the top major service bands. It, too, is a superb musical organization. Its members are of the highest caliber and lead a good life.

A career in any of these military bands is one enjoyed by only a few of the nation's top instrumentalists. Their chairs and honors are the envy of thousands of aspiring instrumentalists who want to play professionally but don't know where to turn for gainful full-time employment.

In addition to these four national military bands, every military base of any size has a post band. The players in these lesser-known organizations enjoy a full-time instrumental music career. Such bands are solid stepping-stones and good advanced training grounds leading to bigger and better things.

Members of these bands go on to arrange, compose, or play in civilian bands of every type. The experience gained from playing in military bands is invaluable.

Municipal Bands

Some large metropolitan areas today employ, from time to time or seasonally, a regular concert band in the old style. The bands are usually most active in summer park programs, fairs, and festivals. Members of these bands are usually full-time professional musicians of top caliber. Membership in the local American Federation of Musicians is usually required.

The library or repertoire of these bands, founded in the great Sousa tradition, includes modern and popular music of the day, show tunes, and traditional classic band titles.

A Career in Band: Vocation or Avocation?

Many seniors graduating from high school bands would like to continue their band work but are unable to see a future in it.

The truth is that literally thousands of high school bandsmen have gone on into exciting careers on the same instrument they played in their high school bands.

Every just-forming or existing band, be it military, municipal, rock, jazz, or dance, needs instrumentalists and replacements. A constant source of such players is the American high school

RAY DICKENSON PHOTO

The foundation of America's instrumental music is truly the American High School Band.

band. There is always room somewhere for a fine instrumentalist. The number and caliber of all professional bands in America is on the increase.

The U.S. Navy School of Music

The U.S. Navy School of Music, in Norfolk, Virginia, was originally a Navy band training center. Today, however, it is a full-fledged conservatory, training young musicians for Army, Navy, Marine, and Air Force bands. This great music school cannot be given too much credit for its important work. It is one of the greatest free opportunities for advanced musical training in the world. The key word is free. One must be in service to take advantage of its opportunity. But it should be pointed out that training in a professional music conservatory or good music school in America or elsewhere is one of the most expensive educations one can seek. Private instrumental lessons, particularly, are very costly. The U.S. Navy School of Music turns out thoroughly trained and musically educated instrumentalists. Its graduates compete successfully with those of any civilian conservatory.

Many high school bandsmen who want to play professionally are unable to continue their education for lack of money. For determined, dedicated, advanced players, the U.S. Navy School of Music is the answer.

The school offers all music classes usually given in a professional conservatory. Application information may be obtained from any recruiting officer of the U.S. Service branches.

The rewards of this important school outweigh any requirements for entry. The student accepted there spends a major part of his entire enlistment commitment period in training in professional music. The school's graduates are in every area of band work, musician's unions, rock, jazz, dance bands, and even symphonic music in America.

XIX

CAREERS AND OPPORTUNITIES IN MUSIC

The Popular Music World

A performer or composer in the rock music field has the best chance of anyone to earn fast, large sums of money. Size of income, in many cases, is unrelated to talent or musicianship. However, many top names and income-earners are fine musicians.

Opportunities for careers in rock music are endless. The field seems to be crowded, but public interest is enormous and still growing. It is also fickle and continually shifting. Yet an ill-paid unknown today may be tomorrow's millionaire.

Country Music

This is an important, growing, and lucrative area of today's pop music scene. The audience for country music has mushroomed in city, metro, suburbs, and country alike. The field is no longer to be discredited as simply "hill-billy." It is a sophisticated, complex industry. Top stars become wealthy and enjoy, in many cases, long-lasting popularity. Many serious musicians of professional training go into the country-music field, for it can pay well. A number of conservatory-trained people have become country-music stars.

Jazz

Many high school bandsmen may look upon jazz as a dated music from a bygone day. But the facts prove otherwise. Bands playing and recording jazz and dixieland have sprouted like mushrooms everywhere. Jazz enjoys cultural status. Many players make good livings playing clubs, festivals, and fairs. They are recording artists. It is important to remember that jazz is America's only original art form. One may hear it in Antwerp or Paris, but it came from the good old U.S.A.

Radio and Television

The radio orchestra musicians of yesteryear have simply moved across the hall into television studios. Band leaders and soloists on television show bands enjoy public exposure unknown in earlier radio days.

Many such bandleaders and sidemen soloists, as a result of all this exposure, have an "in" to movie work of many kinds. It can lead to many areas of professional music.

Recording Artists

Successful recording artists earn fantastic sums of money from hit records. Of course, they may have many titles that never become hits. But the disc, 8-track, and cassette consumer public is tremendous and growing by leaps and bounds. Many recording music performers become famous before they even perform publicly before live audiences.

Fortunately for newcomers to the music scene, New York City is no longer the main or only center of the recording industry. Today any major city has such facilities. Frequently big hits come from unknown recording companies, made by virtually unknown performers.

Nashville, Tennessee, has become, however, one of the most important recording centers in America. All types of stars and sidemen go to Nashville. It is no longer just a string-player's heaven or a place for hill-billy guitarists to sing through their noses on the "Grand Ole Opry." Many of the older, traditional, and established record companies have offices or headquarters and studios there.

Classical and Symphonic Opportunities

Although opportunities for careers in classical and symphonic music are not as numerous as in pop music, they do exist. And the field, too, is growing. As cities become larger in certain regions of the country, they attempt to found their own symphony orchestras.

Every major city in America has its own symphony orchestra today. These musicians are full-time professional players under contract to their orchestras. Most orchestra members are renowned artists or artist-teachers in local colleges or university music departments in off seasons.

Symphony orchestra musicians enjoy a prestige unmatched elsewhere in the total music scene. Smaller cities struggle to found their own symphonies. The students of major symphony artists often have the "in" into these new, smaller city orchestras. By studying with a well-known artist and teacher in a major symphony, the student learns of opportunities in his instrument through his teacher. Every great artist-teacher is a musical source of orchestral members. They are usually the first persons contacted when a certain instrumentalist is needed. For this reason alone, it is important to study with an artist-teacher.

Clinicians and Teachers

Almost every high school and college music department holds music clinics. These are special study-work sessions on a particular instrument or phase of music. The school concerned hosts a "name" clinician, who is usually a visiting teacher, professor, or professional musician.

Frequently the clinician is a member of a major symphony orchestra or a U.S. military service band. In jazz circles or clinics,

Stan Kenton is in great demand for jazz clinics everywhere.

the clinician is usually a jazz or popular orchestra leader or soloist.

These clinics are usually paid employment for the person brought in for the purpose. And even if the pay is not as high as his other income sources, the clinician increases his audience. Eventually he will be paid and repaid many times over, because appearances at clinics around the country or around the world in some cases broaden the name and audience for the clinician.

Judging, or adjudication, of both concert and jazz festivals or contests are income-producing opportunities for musicians. These chances exist on the regional, national and international level.

Such opportunities, taken singly, are not a full-time employment situation. But some "names" are booked so regularly that their full clinic schedules have become almost a full-time paid career. It is a vastly rewarding and enjoyable area of professional music. The influence of these clinicians over young musicians is immeasurable.

The Recording Industry: Artists and Repertoire

Artists and repertoire are perhaps the two most important ingredients in the record world. Without a "name" or star, records do not sell well. And without mass-appeal songs, music, or titles, records do not sell well.

Behind the scenes, however, the recording industry offers opportunities to thousands of music people. Technicians of the sound stage and recording booth and people knowledgeable in music are needed to produce one hit record. Behind every hit record is a vast host of arrangers, composers, managers, booking agents, and financial managers, all deeply involved in the music recording industry.

The radio disc jockey is an important figure in the machinery of popular music. Many such "tune spinners" earn incomes in five and six figures, yet all they appear to do is to play records! Many such people are not required to have a college education or degree; such background, however, is culturally rewarding and adds to the knowledge of the jockey involved.

Musical Research

Some musicians exist on grants from government or educational institutions. It is a pleasant way of life to travel and record native music in its native environment. Many such grant holders receive income from government project funds. Many spend highly enjoyable lives of experience. Recording nationalistic or regional folk music is a common field. The resulting recordings and books on the subject add to the storehouse of world knowledge. They also add to the total income of the researcher involved.

Musicology

Some musicians make successful careers of music history. They teach, lecture, or write on their own special subject area. Some of these musicologists, particularly in the pop music field, are famous, and they enjoy incomes matching their audience size.

Band Directing

This is a large field in music careers. During the 1950's and 1960's, openings for band directors were at every corner. A steadily increasing number of young graduate band directors, however, has created an oversupply today. But opportunities are still in the field. The community college systems could be a logical source or area of opportunity for current band directors and young graduates.

Many school districts prefer to employ local people who have been trained as high school band directors. Many others, however, accept applicants from beyond their immediate area.

Orchestral Conducting

Although it is customary for most major symphonies to get their conductors from abroad, some Americans have won renown, recognition, and positions as symphony conductors. Leonard Bernstein is an example.

Composers

Classical composition is a relatively small field of musical career opportunity, but America's classical composers are growing, both in numbers and stature. Many such men and women are on college faculties, where they teach for a living, but their compositions are increasing their prestige. The classical native American composition field is wide open, but the financial rewards are small.

Music Librarians

One of the little-known but most important career areas in music is that of music librarian. Symphonies, radio and television stations, and the recording industry employ music librarians. As the repertoire and body of music grows, the demand increases for full-time music librarians.

As the body of any given composer's work grows, or any collection begins, the services of an archives librarian become necessary. This is a career area that is very promising in the not-too-distant future.

Music Sales and Service

America abounds with music stores. They all sell music, instruments, and musical supplies and equipment. Many provide some type of warranty service or maintenance. A dependable, careful brass or woodwind repairman can almost command his own price. Such artists are hard to find and badly needed.

Every band and orchestra active in the music world daily requires the services of a good repairman. Often speed and efficient work are crucial to an important performance. There is a great need for skilled men in this area.

The rise in sales of electronic musical instruments and all

their accompanying equipment increases the field of opportunity for music-minded people.

The floor salesman in a music store is more apt to make a sale and a commission or increase his earnings if he can demonstrate the instrument he sells. Band instrument salesmen particularly sell more if they can impressively demonstrate how the instrument should sound.

Summing Up

Music is a vast marketplace, where the arts and every type of musical activity are for sale. The music industry involves more people than any other field of human endeavor. It is a wide, wide world, waiting with open arms for new and talented performers, gifted teachers, technicians, agents, booking agencies, impresarios, promoters, salesmen, repairmen, and stars of tomorrow.

The opportunities for the graduating high school bandsman are vast. If the bandsman wants to make a career in music, he should consider as true and dependable the old adage, "Seek and ye shall find."

Lastly, remember, one does not choose music: music claims its own.

Good luck! And happy hunting in America's musical hunting ground. Fair game is plentiful. There is enough for everybody.

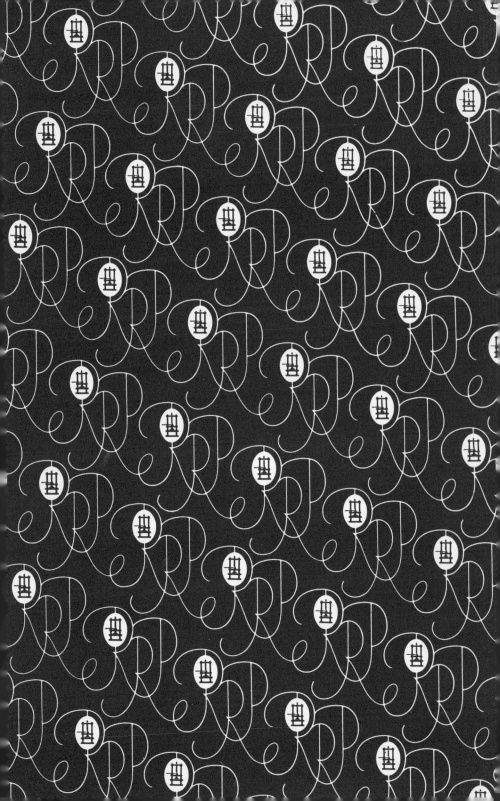